The Annals of Willenhall

Frederick William Hackwood

Alpha Editions

This edition published in 2024

ISBN : 9789367246313

Design and Setting By
Alpha Editions
www.alphaedis.com
Email - info@alphaedis.com

As per information held with us this book is in Public Domain.
This book is a reproduction of an important historical work. Alpha Editions uses the best technology to reproduce historical work in the same manner it was first published to preserve its original nature. Any marks or number seen are left intentionally to preserve its true form.

I.—Its Name and Its Antiquity

Willenhall, vulgo Willnal, is undoubtedly a place of great antiquity; on the evidence of its name it manifestly had its foundation in an early Saxon settlement. The Anglo-Saxon form of the name Willanhale may be interpreted as "the meadow land of Willa"—Willa being a personal name, probably that of the tribal leader, the head of a Teutonic family, who settled here. In the Domesday Book the name appears as Winehala, but by the twelfth century had approached as near to its modern form as Willenhal and Willenhale.

Dr. Oliver, in his History of Wolverhampton, derives the name from Velen, the Sun-god, and the Rev. H. Barber, of Ashby-de-la-Zouch, who tries to find a Danish origin for nearly all our old Midland place-names, suggests the Norse form Vil-hjalmr; or perhaps a connection with Scandinavian family names such as Willing and Wlmer.

Dr. Barber fortifies himself by quoting Scott:—

> Beneath the shade the Northmen came,
> Fixed on each vale a Runic name.
>
> Rokeby, Canto, IV.

Here it may not be out of place to mention that Scandinavian influences are occasionally traceable throughout the entire basin of the Trent, even as far as this upper valley of its feeder, the Tame. The place-name Bustleholme (containing the unmistakable Norse root, "holme," indicating a river island) is the appellation of an ancient mill on this stream, just below Wednesbury. In this connection it is interesting to recall Carlyle's words. In his "Hero Worship," the sage informs us of a mode of speech still used by the barge men of the Trent when the river is in a highly flooded state, and running swiftly with a dangerous eddying swirl. The boatmen at such times will call out to each other, "Have a care! there is the Eager coming!" This, says Carlyle, is a relic of Norse mythology, coming down to us from the time when pagan boatmen on the Trent believed in that Northern deity, Aegir, the God of the Sea Tempest, whose name (as he picturesquely puts it) "survives like the peak of a submerged world." This by the way.

Willenhall, however, was situated outside the Danelagh, the western boundary of which was the Watling Street; indeed, the place nomenclature of this locality affords very few examples which are really traceable to the Danish occupation—an almost solitary specimen being the aforementioned name of Bustleholme, near the Delves.

The etymological derivation which has found most favour in times past is that based on the erroneous Domesday form, Winehala. Perhaps Stebbing Shaw is responsible for this, as in his history of the county, written 1798, he says:—"As Wednesbury is but two miles, and Wednesfield but one mile from hence, it is probable that this name might be changed for that of Winehale, from the Saxon word for victory, when that great battle was fought hereabout in 911."

Of this battle, and the victory or "win" which the founding of Willenhall was supposed to commemorate, some account will be given in the next chapter. But the hypothesis of Shaw, and those who adopted his view, apparently involved the supposition that the earliest mention of Willenhall was of a date subsequent to 911 A.D.; but thanks to the recent researches of our eminent local historiographer, Mr. W. H. Duignan, F.S.A. (of Walsall), that position is no longer tenable.

There is in existence a couple of charters dated A.D. 732 (or 733; certainly before the year 734) which were executed by Ethelbald, King of Mercia, at a place named therein as "Willanhalch."

Mr. Duignan says the Mercian kings frequently reside in this part of their dominions, as at Kingsbury, Tamworth, and Penkridge; probably for the convenience of hunting in Cannock Forest, within the boundaries of which Willenhall was anciently located.

Virtually the two charters are one, the same transaction being recorded by careful and punctilious scribes in duplicate; and their purport was to benefit Mildrith, now commonly called St. Mildreda, one of the grand-daughters of King Penda, and probably one of the few canonised worthies who can be claimed as natives of this county-area. She was the Abbess of Minstrey, in the Isle of Thanet, and "sinful Ethelbald," as he humbly styles himself, remits certain taxes and makes certain grants to her newly-founded abbey, all for the good of his soul. These duplicated documents were published in the original Latin in Kemble's "Codex Diplomaticus" in 1843, by Thorpe in his "Diplomatarium Anglicum" in 1865, and again in Birch's "Chartularium Saxonicum" in 1885.

The internal evidence contained in them is to this effect:—"This was executed on the 4th day of the Kalends of November, in the 22nd year of my reign, being the fifteenth decree made in that place which is called Willanhalch." Not one of these three authorities, although in the habit of doing so wherever they can offer an opinion with any reasonable degree of certainty, has ventured to suggest the modern name and identity of the "place called Willanhalch." But Mr. Duignan, with the ripe knowledge and almost unerring judgment he possesses in such matters, has no hesitation whatever in identifying the place as Willenhall. As he says, there is no other place-name in Mercia, or even in England, which could possibly be represented by Willanhalch.

Undoubtedly there is another Willenhall. It is a hamlet in the parish of Holy Trinity, Coventry, and its name was anciently spelt Wylnhale. But the history of the place is naturally involved in that of the city of Coventry, as the hamlet never had any separate and independent existence like that of our Staffordshire township. Any charter emanating from this place would indubitably be dated "Coventry."

The suggestion of Shaw that the name was changed cannot be entertained for one moment; the Anglo-Saxons were not in the habit of changing place-names, but they were very much addicted to the practice of "calling their lands after their own names." Dr. Willmore, in his "History of Walsall" (p. 30) adopts the now discarded derivation of the name of Willenhall. He says "After the defeat a great feast of rejoicing was held by the Saxons at Winehala, the Hall of Victory, and the event was long celebrated by the national poets."

To identify the "Hall of Victory" with Willenhall the Walsall historian proceeds:—"At Lowhill may still be seen the remains of a large tumulus, while in Wrottesley Park are the vestiges of a large encampment, believed by some authorities to be of Danish construction, and to have been occupied by them about the time of these engagements."

Yet in the next paragraph it is admitted that the Danes never gained a permanent footing in this locality, and that there is scarce a name of purely Danish origin in the neighbourhood.

"Willenhalch," then, may be accepted as signifying in Anglo-Saxon "the meadowland of Willan," Willan (not Willen) being a personal name, and halch being a form of healh, signifying "enclosed land on the banks of a stream," as, for instance, on the Willenhall Brook.

Any ancient place-name terminating in "halch" would, in the course of time, terminate in "hall," a termination now commonly construed as "hall," or "mansion." There is nothing inherently improbable in Willenhall having been a temporary royal residence. King John in much later times had his hunting lodge at Brewood. Bushbury, originally Bishopsbury, was so called because one of the early Mercian bishops is said to have made this place his episcopal residence. Attention has been called to the fact that in this vicinity a number of place-names end in "hall," as Willenhall, Tettenhall, Walsall, Pelsall, and Rushall. The inference drawn is that each of these places marks the settlement of some pioneer Anglican chieftain, or, as Dr. Oliver puts it, the mansion and estate of some Saxon thane.

II.—The Battle of Wednesfield.

Although it cannot be admitted that the Battle of Wednesfield, or the great national victory gained on that occasion, provided Willenhall with its name, the event itself may certainly be regarded as the chief historical episode which has occurred in this immediate vicinity. This was "far back in the olden time" when, says the local poetess—

> The Danes lay camped on Woden's field.

Dr. Willmore, in his "History of Walsall" (p. 30), quotes an authority to the effect that the battle fought at Wednesfield in the year 911 "had the important consequence of freeing England from the attacks of these formidable invaders."

This engagement was one of the many which took place between the Saxon and the Dane for dynastic supremacy. Even the mighty prowess of Alfred the Great had failed to give the quietus to Danish pretensions, and his son, Edward the Elder, was engaged in a life-long struggle with the Danes, in the course of which the Princess Ethelfleda, who was Edward's sister, and Great Alfred's daughter, erected castles at Bridgnorth, Stafford, Warwick, Tamworth, and Wednesbury. Edward the Elder had to combat Welsh invasions as well as Danish aggressiveness, and hence the erection of these castles in Mercia, where most of the minor fighting in that disturbed period occurred. For nine years Ethelfleda fought side by side with her husband Ethelred, Earl of Mercia, in the pitiless struggle; and upon his death, continuing as her brother's viceroy, she proved herself one of the ablest women warriors this country has ever known.

In 910 (the Saxon Chronicle informs us) a battle of more than ordinary moment was fought at Tettenhall. The Danes were returning from a raid, laden with rich spoils, when they were overtaken at this spot by the Angles, on the 5th day of August, and there signally defeated. It was to avenge this disaster that the Danes swooped down the following summer from the north, and met their antagonists exactly on the same day of the year, and almost on the same ground. The latter fact may possibly indicate that there was some strategic importance in the locality. Wednesfield being almost within hail of Tettenhall; though the better informed writers, including Mr. James P. Jones, the historian of Tettenhall, have been led to consider the two battles as one engagement.

As a matter of fact, the exact site of the Tettenhall engagement is not known, yet one historian has not hesitated to represent the nature of the conflict as being "so terrible that it could not be described by the most exquisite pen." It seems to have been an engagement of that old-time ferocity which is so exultantly proclaimed in the ancient war song:—

> We there, in strife bewild'ring,
>   Spilt blood enough to swim in:
> We orphaned many children,
>   We widowed many women.
> The eagles and the ravens
>   We glutted with our foemen:
> The heroes and the cravens,
>   The spearmen and the bowmen.

According to Fabius Ethelwerd it was a national and a most memorable fight which occurred at Wednesfield, where three Danish chieftains fell in the conflict; in support of which statement it is mentioned that the Lows, or monumental burial grounds, of the mighty dead are to be found at Wednesfield and Wrottesley. But Wrottesley is nearer to Tettenhall than to Wednesfield. The number of tumuli which once lay scattered over the entire range of this district may perhaps be accountable for the variations in the mediæval chronicles. As we shall see, while it is well agreed that the country lying between Tettenhall and Wombourn on the one hand, and Wednesfield and Willenhall on the other, was the scene of a great struggle, the details of the conflict vary very materially at the hands of different chroniclers. A valuable collection of old records and historical documents relating to this locality was made by John Huntbach, of Featherstone and Seawall, near Wolverhampton, nephew and pupil to that noted antiquary, Sir William Dugdale. The Huntbach MSS. related more directly to Seisdon; and it was this collection which inspired similar efforts on the part of the Willenhall Antiquary, Dr. Richard Wilkes, and ultimately led to the writing of the Rev. Stebbing Shaw's "History of Staffordshire" (1798–1801).

Speaking of the treatment of the battles of Tettenhall and Wednesfield by the old monkish historians, Huntbach says:—"There is very great reason to confirm their testimony who say the battle was here fought; for there are many tumuli or lows there, that shew some great engagement hereabouts, viz., the North Lowe, the South Lowe, Little Lowe, Horslowe, and Thrombelow.

"The first four being yet visible, the North Lowe, near in lands to croft-lodge, the South Lowe near Mr. Hope's windmill, the great and little lowe in the heath grounds; but Horslowe is not discernible by reason of the coal-works that have been here, only it giveth name to the Horselowe Field, since called Horsehull Field, now Horseley Field.

"And there are not only these, but several others, partly in the way betwixt this place and Tottenhall, as at Low Hill, near Seawall, a very large one, and at Hampton Town; and another which giveth name to a field called Ablow Field, upon which stands a bush now called Isley Cross." Ablow Field covered 40 acres of unenclosed ground near Graiseley Brook, and the tumulus once occupied the site now covered by St. Paul's Church.

Dr. Plot believes the ancient remains in Wrottesley Park to be "those of the old Tettenhall of the Danes, who, having resided there for some time, built themselves this city, or place of habitation, which, in the year 907, was finally demolished by Edward the Elder in a most signal and destructive victory. To revenge this fatal quarrel, another army of Danes collected in Northumbria, and invaded Mercia in the same year, when King Edward, with a powerful force of West Saxons and Mercians overtook them at the village of Wednesfield, near Theotenhall (Tettenhall), and vanquished them again, with much slaughter."

Another account, given by the aforementioned Dr. Wilkes, Willenhall's most eminent son, and no mean authority on such matters, says that:—"In the year 895, King Alfred having by a stratagem forced them to leave Hereford on the Wye, they came up to the River Severn as far as Bridgnorth, then called Quat, Quatbridge, or Quatford, committing great enormities, and destroying all before them. We hear no more of them hereabout for thirteen years, but then they raised a great army and fought two bloody battles with King Edward."

The contemporary Saxon annals tell us that the Danes were beaten in Mercia in 911, but do not say where. Doubtless from time to time the whole plain rang with "the din of battle bray," the shout of exultation, and the groan of pain; with the clash of steel on steel, and the dull thud of mighty battleaxe on shields of tough bull hide, all through that disturbed period. It would appear from a later account that at the earlier engagement of 910, which by this writer has been confidently located between Tettenhall and the Wergs, King Edward was himself in command of the Saxon forces, and that he not only gained a decisive victory, but pursued the enemy for five weeks, following them up in their northern fastnesses beyond the Watling Street, from one Danish village to another, burning and utterly wasting every one of them as they had been mere hornets' nests.

At the encounter of the following year (A.D. 911) the Danes, after a great pillaging expedition, having strongly posted themselves at Wednesfield, little advantage was gained by either side after many hours of hard fighting, till at last the Saxons were reinforced by Earl Kenwolf. Victory then fell to the Saxons.

This Kenwolf, who is said to have been the greatest notable of the locality, and seated on a good estate at Stowe Heath, was mortally wounded in the fray; and on the opposite side there fell Healfden and Ecwills, two Danish kings; Ohter and Scurfar, two of their Earls; a number of other great noblemen and generals, among them Othulf, Beneting, Therferth, Guthferth, Agmund, Anlaf the Black, and Osferth the tax-gatherer, and a host of men. The name of a third slaughtered king, Fuver, is given by another old chronicler. It is to the quality rather than to the quantity of the slain that the locality is indebted for the number of tumuli on which so much of this superstructure of quasi-history seems to be raised.

The historians who restrict themselves to "two" kings specify the North Lowe at Wednesfield as the sepulchral monument of one, and the South Lowe of the other. "There was," says Shaw, the county historian, "a little to the south of the Walsall Road, half a mile south-west of the village of Nechels, a great low called Stowman Hill."

Dr. Plot, writing in 1686, declares "the bank above Nechels, where now is a stone pit, Stowman Low, now removed to mend the roads, and Northfield, to be the genuine remains; but the bank where the windmill stood was a hard rock, several yards below the surface of the earth, and there was nothing remarkable found upon the removing of Stowman Low, so that all this is uncertainty."

Although the precise location of the Tettenhall battleground has always puzzled the antiquaries, there are, says one authority, "three lows on the common between Wombourn and Swin, placed in a right line that runs directly east and west, and about half a mile to the north of them is another, by the country people called Soldiers' Hill. They are all large and capable of covering a great number of dead bodies.

"There cannot be the least doubt but this place was the scene of action, for King Edward, to perpetuate the memory of this signal victory, I presume, here founded a church, called by the name of the place Wonbourn, now Wombourn; and took this whole parish out of the parish of Tettenhall, which, before this battle, extended as far as the forest of Kinver." It may be added, for whatever such support is worth, that in times past a number of ancient weapons have been dug up at Wombourne.

Coming to the latest and most reliable authority, Mr. W. H. Duignan, of Walsall, here is what he writes in his admirable work, "Staffordshire Place Names," under the heading "Low Hill," which is the name of an ancient estate at Bushbury:—

"Huntbach the antiquary, wrote in the 17th century that there was then a very large tumulus here. Much, if not the whole of it, has been since destroyed. The hill is lofty and a place likely to be selected for the burial of some prehistoric magnate. In 911 a battle was fought between the Saxons and the Danes, called in the Chronicles the battle of Tettenhall, but which was really waged on Wednesfield Heath (now Heath Town).

"The dead were buried as usual under mounds, which in Huntbach's time still remained, and were known as North Low, South Low, the Little Low, the Great Low, Horselow, Tromelow, and Ablow (many of these names survive), besides others which had then disappeared. It is therefore difficult to say whether the low here was a prehistoric tumulus or a battle mound."

Dr. Langford, in his "Staffordshire and Warwickshire" (p. 177), writing less than forty years ago, says that "a large number of tumuli exist near Wednesfield"; but the utilitarianism of the farmer and the miner would make it difficult to find many of these grass-crowned records on the Willenhall side of the battleground now. Dr. Windle, in his able work, "Remains of the Prehistoric Age in England" (published in 1904) gives a list of existing Barrows and Burial-mounds in this country, including some nine or ten in Staffordshire, but makes no mention of Wednesfield, Wombourne, or Tettenhall.

II.—The Saxon Settlement

Fourteen or fifteen centuries ago the cluster of places which we now know as the town of Wolverhampton, and the numerous industrial centres grouped around it, were then primitive Saxon settlements, each of them peopled by the few families that claimed kinship with each other.

These embryo townships were dotted about the clearings which had been made in the thick primeval forest with which the whole face of England was then covered, save only where the surface was barren hill or undrained swamp. Does not the terminal "field," in such a place-name as Wednesfield, literally mean "feld," or the woodland clearing from which the timbers had been "felled"? Each settlement, whether called a "ham" (that is, a home), or a "tun" (otherwise a town), was a farmer-commonwealth, cultivating the village fields in common; each was surrounded by a "mark," or belt of waste land, which no man might appropriate, and no stranger advance across without first blowing his horn to give timely notice of his approach. Remnants of these open unappropriated lands may be traced by such place-names as Wednesfield "Heath," and Monmore "Green."

At the outset each settlement at its foundation was independent of, and co-equal with, the others; Saxon society being founded on a system of family groupings, and a government of the ancient patriarchal type.

All questions of government and public interest were settled by the voice of the people in "moot," or open-air meeting, assembled beneath the shelter of some convenient tree. Our ancestors were an open-air, freedom-loving people, who mistrusted walls and contemned fortifications. In course of time, however, the exigencies of their environment—the aggressiveness of neighbours and foreigners, the incursions of invaders and marauders—materially modified their views, and changed their habits in this respect; and so it came about in the scheme of national defence that the temple-crowned hill of Woden became Woden's burh (now Wednesbury), a hill fortified by deep ditch and high stockade.

Presently the family tie gave way to the lordship, as certain chiefs, under the stress of circumstances, acquired domination over others, and hence arose the manor or residential lordship, the head of which took pledges for the fidelity of those below him, and in turn became responsible for them to the king above him—a system of mutual inter-dependence from the head of the state downwards. Under these new conditions Stow Heath became the head of a Saxon manor, in which were involved Willenhall, Wolverhampton, Bilston, Wednesfield, Eccleshall, and a number of other village settlements. Some of these, however, were in the Hundred of Seisdon, and some in the Hundred of Offlow—a "hundred" being originally the division of a county that contained a hundred villages.

The unregenerate Teuton was a pirate and a plunderer; the settled Saxon became an oversea trader and trafficker. The Anglo-Saxon merchant of later and more settled times, raised by his wealth to the dignity of a thane, became a landed man, and a lord over his fellows. Herein we have the transition from a free village community to a Saxon manor.

At Wolverhampton was seated one Wolfric, said to have been an ancestor of Wolfgeat, and a relation to Wulfruna; his manor house was situated on the slope of the hill between the present North Street and Waterloo Road—doubtless a large rambling mansion of low elevation, built of heavy timbers on a low plinth of boulders and hewn stones.

Here at Hantun he kept his state—such as the luxury of the age permitted to him. Seated in his great oaken hall, with its heavy roof timbers, at the close of each day he drank deep draughts with his guests and his numerous servants, in the flaring light of odorous resin torches stuck in iron staples along the walls. The smoke from his fire of logs escaped as lazily as it might through an aperture in the roof. The earthen floor was strewn with rushes, more or less clean as it was littered by the refuse of few or more feasts. The only furniture consisted of a long trestle table, with rude benches of oak on each side; the whole effort at ornamentation being limited to trophies of war and the chase hanging upon the walls. Such, in brief, was the home life of a great thane.

It will be observed that Wednesfield and Wednesbury at least were founded by the Saxons in their pagan days; that is before their acceptance of the White Christ, which was towards the close of the seventh century. Tradition hath it that at the Anglian advent into this district, the worship of Woden was first set up in a grove at Wednesfield. Here was first fixed the Woden Stone, the sacred altar on which human sacrifices were offered of that dread Teutonic deity, Woden.

It was carved with Runic figures—for was not Woden the inventor of the Runic characters? In sacrificing, the priest, at the slaying of the victim, took care to consecrate the offering by pronouncing always the solemn formula, "I devote thee to Woden!"

Part of the blood was then sprinkled on the worshippers, part on the sacred grove; the bodies were then either burnt on the altar or suspended on trees within this mystic grove. Later, when some advance had been made by the hierarchy, the Woden Stone was removed from the Wednesfield grove to be erected within the temple of Woden at Wednesbury.

There are other evidences of pagan practices to be discovered in Staffordshire place-names. Tutbury is said to derive its name from Tuisto, the Saxon god who gave the name to Tuesday, as Woden lent his to Wednesday; and Thursfield from Thor, the deity worshipped on Thursday. There is also Thor's cave, still so-called, in the north of this county (see "Staffordshire Curiosities," p. 159), and other similar reminders of Anglo-Saxon paganism.

It is not outside the bounds of possibility that a third local place-name is traceable to the personality of Woden. Sedgley may be derived from Sigge's Lea, and Sigge was the real name of the Teutonic conqueror who, in overrunning north-west Europe, assumed the name of Woden for the sake of prestige—he was the founder of Sigtuna, otherwise Sigge's town, in Sweden. In the science of English place-names it is well-known that while hills and streams and other natural phenomena were allowed to retain their old British names (as Barr, "a summit," and Tame, "a flood water"), towns, villages, and other political divisions were very generally renamed by the Saxon conquerors, the places in many instances being called after the personal names of their owners.

Here are some local illustrations of place-names conferred by the Anglian invaders when they had conquered and appropriated the territory.

Arley, otherwise Earnlege, was "the Eagle's ley."

Bilston signifies "the town of Bil's folk."

Blakenhall was "the hall of Blac."

Bloxwich was "the village of Bloc": as Wightwick was "Wiht's village."

Bushbury was "the Bishop's burg."

Chillington was originally "Cille's town."

Codsall was "Code's hall."

Darlaston was once "Deorlaf's town."

Dunstall, otherwise Tunstall, was "an enclosed farmstead," half a mile outside the ancient boundary of Cannock Forest.

Essington was "the town of the descendants of Esne."

Ettingshall was "the hall of the Etri family."

Featherstone seems to have been "Feader's stone." According to a charter of the year 994 there was then a large stone called the "Warstone," to mark the boundary of this place.

Hatherton, or Hagathornden, signifies "the hill of the hawthorn."

Kinvaston was perhaps "Cyneweald's town." Dr. Olive in his "History of Wolverhampton Church," says that being originally a place of consequence. Kinvaston was placed at the head of the Wolverhampton prebends.

Moseley was the "mossy or marshy lea": as Bradley the "broad lea"; and Bentley was the "lea of bent" or reedy grass.

Newbolds, an ancient farm in Wednesfield, is an Anglo-Saxon name, "niwe bold," and it pointed out "the new house."

Ogley Hay, now called Brownhills, was originally Ocginton, or "Ocga's town."

Pelsall may be translated "Peol's Hall."

Pendeford was once "Penda's ford."

Scotlands were "the corner-lands," this hamlet being at the corner of a triangular piece of land, bounded on all sides by ancient roads.

Seisdon was probably "the Saxon's Hill."

Showells, or Sewalls, at Bushbury, on the confines of Cannock Forest, was the place where "scarecrows" (as the name probably means) were set up or shown on hedgetops to prevent the deer passing from the Forest on to enclosed or cultivated land.

Stowe, a name signifying an enclosed or "stockaded" place, was another seat of a great thane; or it might have been the residential portion of the large manor or lordship already alluded to.

Tettenhall was possibly Tetta's hall; or, more probably, "Spy hall," otherwise a watch tower.

Tromelow, commonly called Rumbelows, a farm on the site of one of the Wednesfield lows, is a name that may literally mean "the burial mound of the host." The corruption Rumbelow is probably made out of the phrase "At Tromelowe."

Wergs (The), through many transformations from Wytheges to Wyrges, is "the withy hedges."

Wobaston, an estate in Bushbury, was anciently "Wibald's town."

Wombourne was the "bourne (or brook) in the hollow."

Wolverhampton was at first Heantune, or Hamtun, otherwise the "High town," to which name was prefixed soon after the year 994 that of Wulfrun, a lady of rank who gave great possessions to the Church; and hence was evolved the more distinctive name, Wulfrunhamtun, since modified into its present form.

Although some of these names (as Showells, formerly Sewall) may not date quite back to the Saxon period, most of them may be accepted as present-day evidences of the great Teutonic descent upon this Midland locality. One of the very few Celtic place-names retained from the previous occupiers is Monmore, which in the tongue of the ancient Britons signified "the boggy mere."

IV.—The Founding of Wulfruna's Church, 996, A.D.

After the advent of Christianity, the new religion was gradually advanced throughout the land by the settlement of priest-missioners in the various localities. Where the missionary settled on the invitation, or under the protection of a thane, or "lord," that lordship was formed into a parish. Thus some parishes doubtless became co-terminous with the old manors. Owing, however, to the many changes of jurisdiction in the course of succeeding centuries, it is difficult to find instances of parish and manor of identical area in this locality. Bescot was a manor within the parish of Walsall; Bloxwich and Shelfield were anciently members of the manor of Wednesbury, though now included in Walsall; Bentley, at the Norman Conquest, was part of the manor of Willenhall, then belonging to Wolverhampton Church; while Dunstall was a member of the King's manor of Stow Heath. Tettenhall parish originally included as many as a dozen manors and townships.

England is made up of some ten thousand parishes, each with its parish church, around which for a thousand years has revolved the social and political, as well as the whole religious life of the place. The parish is our unit of local government, and the history of a town is usually a history of the parish.

But Willenhall never was a parish. It is merely a member of a parish—of the extensive, the straggling, and loosely-knit parish of Wolverhampton. In Wolverhampton, three miles away, was located the mother church, to which it owed spiritual allegiance, and there was situated the Vestry for parochial assemblies, and all else that stood for self-government throughout the centuries. And those were the centuries when Church and State were indissolubly bound together; when a dominant church claimed, and was recognised as having an inalienable share in the government of the people. Hence it will transpire in these pages that for centuries the story of Willenhall was involved in the ecclesiastical history of Wolverhampton.

The ancient parish of Wolverhampton lies widely dispersed and very detached, containing no less than 17 townships and hamlets, all subject to the collegiate church in matters ecclesiastical, though in many cases being distinct in matters secular. How broken the area is may be noted in the case of Pelsall, which is cut off from the mother parish by Bloxwich, a hamlet in Walsall parish.

Willenhall is one among several other neighbouring places that, from the earliest period of England's acceptance of Christianity, had its fate inseparably linked with that of Wolverhampton. In the giving way of paganism before the steady advances of the new religion, progress in this immediate part of the kingdom was marked by the founding of Tettenhall

Church (A.D. 966), followed thirty years afterwards by Lady Wulfruna's further efforts at evangelisation in the setting up at Hampton (or High Town) of another Christian church.

This was in the reign of Ethelred the Unrede, which was a period sadly troubled by the aggressions of the Danes; and it is believed that Wulfruna (or Wulfrun) had designed to found a monastery, though as early as the time of Edward the Confessor, or within a century of its institution, her establishment is found to be a Collegiate Church.

With this accession of dignity, and in grateful recognition of the lady's pious munificence, the town became known as Wulfrun's Hampton, now modified in Wolverhampton.

Of Wulfruna herself but little is known. Whether she was sister of King Edgar, as some suppose, or the widow of Aldhelm, Duke of Northumberland, cannot be decided. It is known, however, that she was a lady of rank, and was captured when Olaf, in command of a Viking host, took Tamworth by storm. Hampton did not bear her name until some years after her death.

In founding her noble church at Wolverhampton, Wulfruna endowed it with thirteen estates, including lands in Willenhall, Wednesfield, Pelsall, Essington, Hilton, Walsall, Featherstone, Hatherton, Kinvaston, Bilston, and Arley. Willenhall being only three miles away from Wolverhampton, and being also for a long time ecclesiastically incorporated with it, its history at many points cannot be detached from that of the mother parish.

The wording of the charter by which the gift was made is quaintly interesting. It sets forth that: "In the year 996, from the Passion of our said Lord and Saviour, Jesus Christ," Sigeric, Archbishop of Canterbury, "with the Lord's flock of servants unceasingly serving God," have granted a privilege "to the noble matron and religious woman Wulfruna," in "order that she may attain a seat in heaven," and that "for her mass may be said unceasingly for ever" in the "ancient monastery of Hamtun."

The Charter (inter alia) grants "ten hides of land for the body of my husband," and another "ten hides of land" for the offences of her "Kinsman Wulfgeal" lest he should hear in the judgment the "dreaded" sentence, "Go away from me," &c. A third "ten hides" of land are granted on account of "my sole daughter Elfthryth," who "has migrated from the world to the life-giving airs."

Mr. Duignan, who has made a close study of the Charter, says "the limits of the parishes and of the townships included in the grant are now precisely what they were a thousand years ago."

The boundaries of the lands conferred by the noble benefactress are set forth with much precision, as in the noting of brooks and fords, of parks and woods, of fields and lanes and lands; and in very few cases has Mr. Duignan failed to recognise the old names and identify them with the modern appellations of the places meant, among the latter being Willenhall, Wednesfield, Pelsall, Hilton, Ogley Hay, Hatherton, Cannock, Moseley Hole, Twyford, Walsall, &c.

The original Charter has not been heard of since 1646, when it was supposed to be copied by Sir William Dugdale into his monumental work, the "Monasticon," assisted by Roger Dodsworth, a joint editor with him. If it is still in existence Mr. Duignan assumes it is in the possession of the Dean and Chapter of the Royal Chapel of Windsor, with which the Deanery of Wolverhampton was united—as will be seen later. The formal parts of the deed are in Latin, and the descriptions of the properties are in Anglo-Saxon, which makes it an interesting study of place-names.

Wolverhampton church, dedicated to St. Mary, was a collegiate establishment, with a dean as president, and a number of prebendaries or canons who were "secular" priests, and not brethren of any of the regular "orders of monks."

All the privileges which the College possessed in Lady Wulfruna's lifetime were afterwards confirmed by Edward the Confessor, and subsequently by William the Conqueror.

* * * * *

The dedication of Wulfruna's church and its consecration by Sigeric, the archbishop, have been described in verse by a local poetess. This was Mrs. Frank P. Fellows, a daughter of the famous Sir Rowland Hill, and once resident at Goldthorn Hill. Her husband was a native of Wolverhampton, a distinguished public servant, connected with the Admiralty, a Knight of St. John of Jerusalem, an antiquarian and a scientist. In a book of his published poems appear portraits of himself and his wife.

Mrs. Fellows (whose mother, Lady Hill, was a daughter of Joseph Pearson, Esq., J.P., of Graiseley), also wrote poems—some of which appeared in "Punch," some in "Belgravia," and some in other magazines—and published a small book of verse in 1857.

It is from one long piece, entitled "Fancies by the Fire," in which the long retrospect of Wolverhampton's ancient history unrolls itself before the imagination of the poetess, that the following extracts are taken. After a description of the battle of Wednesfield, we read:—

> The Princess Wulfruna heard the deeds,
> Told by the fire in her stately hall.
>> Alas! then said the gentle dame,
>> It grieves me sore such things should be.
>> Now, by the Christ that died on tree,
>> The Christ that died for them and me,
>> These heathen souls shall all be free
>> From sin, and pain of Purgat'ry;
>> In token of our victory,
>> Where masses shall be sung and said,
>> And prayers told for the restless dead
>> That wander still on Woden's Plain—
>> It shall be raised in Mary's name.

The noble lady with her train, and accompanied by the Archbishop Sigeric, pays a visit of inspection to the locality she designs thus to honour, passing beneath the shade of "the forest trees of Theotanhall" on her way—

> And as they passed thro' Dunstall Wood,
> And stopped to drink where a streamlet fell,
> Then said the lady fair and good
> Here will I build a wayside well.
> Now Hampton town before them lay.
> But first they sought out Woden's plain,
> Where lay the bleached bones of the slain.

After the Archbishop had offered up a prayer for the dead—

> At length they stood upon the height
> That rises over Hampton town;
> There, amid knight, and dame, and priest,
> The Princess Wulfrune laid the stone,
> The first stone on the holy fane.

Then solemnly the pious lady removed from her royal brows the golden coronet that hitherto had graced it, and put in place of it a crown of thorns, saying—

> It were ill done that I have worn
> A golden crown, while Jesus sweet
> For my sake wore a crown of thorn;
> And here I dedicate my days
> To Him until my life be sped.

Thus far the foundation of the mother church—much more of the town's history follows in like strain.

* * * * * *

Willenhall was slightly connected with another religious foundation. In the year 1002 Burton Abbey was founded by Wulfric Spott, Earl of Mercia. This establishment was richly endowed with lands, not only in Staffordshire, but also with estates in Derbyshire and Warwickshire.

The names of the various places included in this munificent grant afford a very interesting study in Saxon nomenclature. For instance, in the Second Indorsement of the Charter conferring the noble gift, we may be interested to discover that "2 hides of land in Wilinhale," lying in "Offalawe Hundred" are among the properties donated to this great Staffordshire Monastery.

V.—The Collegiate Establishment

We cannot be too insistent on the close connection long subsisting between Willenhall and Wolverhampton owing to the fact of the former being a part of Wulfruna's endowment of her collegiate church.

Wulfruna's foundation consisted of a dean, eight prebendaries or canons, and a sacrist. The dean was the president of this chapter, or congregation of clergy, whose duty was to chant the daily service. The sacrist was also a cleric, but his duties were more generally concerned with the college establishment.

A prebendary, it may be explained, is one who enjoys a prebend or canonical portion; that is, who receives in right of his place, a share out of the common stock of the church for his maintenance. Each prebend of Wolverhampton church was endowed with the income arising from the lands from which it took its name; as, the prebend of Willenhall. In the course of time the tithes derivable from these lands became alienated.

Sampson Erdeswick, whose history of this county was commenced in 1593, says the foundation was effectuated in 970 by King Edgar, at the request of his dying sister, Wulfruna.

"She founded a chapel of eight portionaries (is the way Erdeswick puts it) whom, by incorporation, she made rector of that parish (Wolverhampton) to receive the tithes in common, but devisable by a yearly lot. The head or chief of these she made patron to them all, and sole ordinary of that whole parish."

The foundation was designated the "royal free church of Wolverhampton," the term "free" signifying that it was free of the ordinary supervision of the ecclesiastical authorities, being exempt from both episcopal jurisdiction and the papal supremacy. Indeed, it had been better for the church had it been less free, for in the time of King John the debaucheries and gross immoralities of these undisciplined parochial clergy brought much discredit upon the priestly college.

The dean and the prebends had special seats or stalls in the choir of the church; the sacrist had no stall, neither had he any voice in the chapter. In modern times (1811) the sacrist has become the perpetual curate of the parish.

It will be noted that the head of this college of seculars was styled the "sole ordinary" of the parish, which is equivalent to saying he was invested with judicial powers therein like a bishop in a diocese. He had authority cum omnimoda jurisdictione, and was exempt not only from the episcopal overlordship of Coventry and Lichfield by express composition, but also by papal bull from the legates and delegates of Rome for ever. In fact, so independent was the foundation made at the outset, it remained for centuries subject only to the royal authority of the Majesty of England, and under it to the perpetual visitation of the Keepers of the Great Seal for the time being.

In the year 1338, Edward III. confirmed the charter of the church as a royal free chapter, giving the Dean the jurisdiction of a Court Leet, and a copyhold Court Baron, to be called the Deanery Court of Wolverhampton. About this time, too, the church was rebuilt on more spacious and magnificent lines. Mrs. Fellows, in her topographical rhyme, previously quoted, sings of the erection of the tower

> In the third Edward's time.

The college then consisted of the ten members of the foundation just mentioned, augmented by other ministers and officers necessary for conducting so large an establishment, the prebendaries being officially mentioned in this order:—(1) Wolverhampton; (2) Kinvaston; (3) Featherstone; (4) Hilton; (5) Willenhall; (6) Monmore; (7) Wobaston; (8) Hatherton.

By the fifteenth century Chantries had been founded, and chapels erected therefor, at Willenhall, Bilston, Pelsall, and at Hatherton; and in further depreciation of the mother church, King Edward IV., about 1465, with a desire to enrich the Collegiate Church of St. George, at Windsor, annexed Wolverhampton to that chapel royal.

In Protestant times the daily services were performed by the sacrist and the readers, the prebendaries officiating on Sundays in rotation, according to a set cycle. The time set out for the prebendary of Willenhall commenced on the Sunday after Ash Wednesday; till eventually exemption was purchased by the payment of a small fee to the Perpetual Curate.

In olden times it was a common practice to carve the choir seats. The prebendal stalls in Wolverhampton church were marked with heraldic shields charged with simple ordinaries, in the following manner:—the following manner:—

ON THE SOUTH SIDE.

1. The Dean. On a fess, three roundels.

2. Prebendary of Featherstone. A pale cotised.

3. Prebendary of Willenhall. A Chevron.

4. Prebendary of Wobaston. A Chevron.

5. Prebendary of Hatherton. A pale cotised.

ON THE NORTH SIDE.

6. Prebendary of Kinvaston. (Stall removed.)

7. Prebendary of Hilton. A Chevron renversé.

8. Prebendary of Monmore. A Chevron.

To assist in the identification of the various estates chargeable with the provisions of the prebends, or canonical portions, it may be useful to give here a brief account of a perambulation of the Wolverhampton parish boundaries made in 1824.

It was a regular Rogation ceremony of "beating the bounds" and occupied three whole days, so widely scattered is this extensive, far-reaching parish. It will be observed that the Hatherton here dealt with is not the Staffordshire village of that name, two miles north-west of Cannock. Wobaston, it will be remembered, has previously been mentioned as situated in Bushbury; while Monmore Green is still a well-known place-name. The other names occur in self-explanatory context. The detailed account of this perambulation, of which the following is but a summary, will be found in the appendix to Dr. Oliver's "History":—

On Monday, May 24th, the churchwardens and their party assembled at the Rev. Thomas Walker's, and proceeded to a cottage near the eighth milestone on the Stafford Road, and at the well in the cottage garden there, the Gospel was read for the first time. (It was the custom at these Rogation processionings to read the Gospel under trees—especially those growing near to some reputed "holy" well—located on or near a parish boundary, hence their name "Gospel trees.")

From thence a lane near the third milestone on the same road led the procession to Kinvaston, where the Gospel was read at an Elder in the fold-yard of a house of a Mrs. Wooton. Then the procession went to Hatherton, the seat of the late Moreton Walhouse, where the Gospel was again read on the site of an old well. Proceeding to Hilton, the seat of the Vernons, the Gospelling was repeated within the gates fronting the house.

Crossing the Cannock Road, the Gospel was read for the fifth and last time, that day, under an oak tree in the road near the house of Mr. W. Price, of Featherstone.

On the second day, May 25th, the parishioners assembled as before, and proceeded direct to Wednesfield, where the Gospel was read in the Chapel, the clerk being in readiness at the door to receive the procession. Thence the perambulation was continued to Essington, where the common was found to be enclosed; the Gospel was read a second time there at the Goswell Bush, which, standing in the Bloxwich Road, was found to be surrounded by a new growth of trees. (Just previous to this period there had been a rage for enclosing commons—the people's lands.) Turning back, the party proceeded to Pelsall, where the Gospel was read the third and last time, that day, in the Chapel there.

On the third day, which was Thursday, May 27th, the assembly was made at the Swan Inn, and the procession was formed there. The way was led straight to Willenhall, where the Gospel was read for the first time in the Chapel, the expectant clerk being there in readiness to perform the duty. From thence the perambulation was continued to Park Brook, which was crossed; returning, the way was taken to Bentley Hall, the seat of Edward Anson, Esq., where the second reading of the Gospel was taken at an elder bush at the back of the house. (Elders seem to have taken the place of the ancient "Gospel oaks" in this locality.)

From Willenhall the party next proceeded to Bilston, where the third reading of the Gospel was performed within the Chapel of that township.

From thence a move was made to Bradeley Hall, then in the occupation of Mr. Nailer, at the bottom of whose garden was the site of an old well, which had once been a bath, and here the Gospelling was again celebrated.

The procession was then resumed through Bilston by Catchem's Corner, Goldthorne Hill, and the Penn Road, to St. John's Chapel, otherwise known as the New Church, within which the Gospel was ceremonially read for the last time. This concluded the perambulation, and an entry of its various details were duly entered in the Parish Book, and signed by Tho. Walker, minister, and Wm. Buckle and Jos. Smart, the two churchwardens.

VI—Willenhall at the Norman Conquest (1066–1086).

After the Norman invasion of 1066 it took a number of years to complete the conquest of the country. It was not till 1086 that the "Domesday" Book was compiled—written evidence of a settlement of the land question which, it was fondly hoped (and expressed in the name), would last till "Domesday"!

The Domesday Book was a great national land register in which was entered a record of every acre of land in England, its condition, its ownership, and annual value at that time. For on land ownership alone then depended not only the amount of the national revenue, but the strength of the national defences. Willenhall, wrongly written by the Domesday scribes as Winehala, is returned as being in the Hundred of Offlow, and having an area of 2,168 acres.

Of this acreage 3 hides belonged to the old domains of the Crown, like Bilston and Wednesbury (having formerly formed part of the dominions of the Saxon kings), while but two hides of Willenhall land belonged to Wolverhampton church. It is believed that the King's manorial portion took with it Bentley, with its 1,650 acres.

Anyway, Willenhall having belonged originally to the ancient Mercian kings, and having been held in succession by all the Saxon kings of England to Edward the Confessor and Harold II., naturally passed as a royal manor, or rather, a portion thereof, into the hands of the Conqueror, being set down among the Crown lands as of "ancient demesne."

The Domesday Book also sets down among the possessions of the Canons of Wolverhampton 2,200 acres in Wednesfield, 1,194 acres in Pelsall, both in the same Hundred; 3,396 acres in Wolverhampton, 3,912 acres in Arley, and 6,377 acres, a part of Bushbury, are set down in Seisdon Hundred; the Essington portion of Bushbury, once belonging to the Countess Godiva, is reckoned in Cuddlestone Hundred, in which are also given the four other portions of Wolverhampton, namely Hilton, Hatherton, Kinvaston, and Featherstone.

Since the eleventh century the boundaries of the Hundreds of Offlow and Cuddlestone have been altered. As to the Arley estate, that was lost to the canons ere another century had elapsed—by 1172 had escheated to the Crown.

The present-day acreage of Wolverhampton parish is no less than 17,449; made up of 3,396 acres in Wolverhampton proper, 1,845 in Bilston, and 1,650 in Bentley, a total of 6,891 acres in Seisdon Hundred; thus leaving 10,608 acres to constitute Hilton (two manors, since united into one) Hatherton, Kinvaston, Featherstone, and Hocintune. The last-named was a manor which, at that time, probably lay between Hilton and Hatherton, within Wolverhampton; the name is obsolete.

These ten estates, comprising Wolverhampton, Willenhall (part of), Arley (part of), Bushbury (part of), Hilton (part of), Pelsall, Wednesfield, Cote (near Penn), Haswic (near Newcastle), and Hocintune (now obsolete), were in 1086 held by the Canons of Wolverhampton under Sampson, the highly favoured royal Chaplain, to whom the Conqueror had presented this fief. For the purposes of comparison it may be mentioned that there were then eighteen holdings in Staffordshire, occupying 567 hides, and valued at about £516. Sampson's fief extended to 26½ hides of this, and was estimated as being worth £8 2s. a year.

This Sampson, who has been incorrectly styled the first Dean of Wolverhampton, was a Canon of Bayeux, and though a king's chaplain, was not ordained a priest till nine years after the Conqueror's death, when Rufus made him Bishop of Worcester. Bishop Sampson subsequently gave the Church of Wolverhampton to his Cathedral Monastery of Worcester. He also held the neighbouring estates at Bilbrook and Tettenhall as the superior of the priests of Tettenhall College.

Willenhall, in the great survey, is recorded to have contained, as previously stated, three hides belonging to the King, and two hides belonging to the church—a hide of land in Saxon measurement was a variable quantity from 200 to 600 acres, according to the locality, but generally it was accounted so much as would serve to maintain a family—together with one acre of meadow, and a carucate (which was a measure of about 100 acres of "carved" land) employing three ploughs. The annual value of Willenhall is set down at 20s. The population consisted of eight families, or, as the return puts it, five bordars and three villeins.

A bordar, or boor, was a squatter living in a hut or cottage on the borders of a manor, having attached a little patch of land, the rent of which was paid to the lord of the manor in the shape of poultry, eggs, and small produce. A villein, or serf, was to all intents and purposes a slave, at the absolute disposal of the lord, except that he could not be detached from the soil on which he was born. While the bordar, or cottager, was resident in the manor more or less on sufferance, the villein was there of right, and was in that sense the superior of the bordar. The villein certainly might not go away from Willenhall, nor get married, nor buy and sell oxen, nor grind corn, without the express permission of the lord of the manor; yet he was not so badly off as all this would make it appear to our modern ideas. People seldom travelled in those days, money was little used, life was exceedingly primitive, and wants were very few and very simple.

Staffordshire at that time was in a chronic state of poverty, an insurrection in the county having been suppressed in 1069 with the Conqueror's customary severity, thousands of the wretched hinds having been slaughtered, the county desolated and the Midlands depopulated.

Bilston was but a cluster of mud huts inhabited by swineherds; and it is probable Willenhall was a similar little centre of boor life in the next woodland clearing a little further along the purling brooklet, and near its junction with Beorgitha's Stream, as the Tame was then called. The entire population of the county was purely agrarian, the villeins and boors altogether numbering about 2,800; or on an average of one labourer to each 167 acres of land registered in Domesday Book. The subsequent history of the two parts of Willenhall will have to be traced separately.

The two hides set down as ecclesiastical property have remained in the possession of the church throughout. Erdeswick, writing his history of this county in 1593, states that within the jurisdiction of the Dean and Chapter of Wolverhampton there were then "nine several leets, whereof eight belong to the church. The custos, lately called the Dean, is lord of the borough of Wolverhampton, Codsall, Hatherton, and Pelsall in com. Stafford; and of Lutley in com. Wigorn; hath all manner of privileges belonging to the View of Frankpledge (that is, the administration of criminal justice, &c.), to Felons' goods, Deodands, Escheats, Marriage of Wards, and Clerks of the Weekly Markets, rated at £150 per annum, and in the total is valued worth £300 per annum.

"Each of the other portionaries (continues Erdeswick) have a several leet; whereof

Kinvaston is reputed worth	£100
Wobaston	£100
Wilnall	£100
Fetherston	£80
Hilton	£70
Monmore	£70
Hatherton	£40

"And the sacrist to attend them in capitulo, £40"—by no means a poor salary in those days for such duties as the secretarial and managerial work to a Chapter.

As to the three hides of Willenhall in the King's Manor of Stow Heath, here is its later history as recorded by Dr. Vernon, a historiographer who made some additions to Sampson Erdeswick's history:—

> "In Willenhall is a manor called Stowheath, with a court baron and court leet. Several lands there held by copy from that lords thereof: four closes, called bundles, held of this manor, and were, in 1729, confirmed by John, Lord Gower, and Peter Giffard, lords of the manor of Stowheath; which four closes, with four others, were sold about 1748 by Mr. Lane to Admiral Anson, together with three tenements in Bloxwich, with all the manor lands, tithes, hall, and park, &c., called Bentley, adjoining to Willenhall, for £13,500."

As to the adjoining hamlet, it may be mentioned that Domesday Book formally recorded the canons of Wolverhampton to possess "five hides of Wednesfelde; the arable land is three carucates; that there are six villeins, and six bordars, who have six carucates; and that there is a wood in which cattle are pastured, half a mile long and three furlongs broad."

Such was life in Willenhall and Wednesfield at the Norman period, both places being then overshadowed in more senses than one by the severely protected royal preserves of Cannock Forest. We may picture the few hinds constituting the scanty population, tenanting cottages which were mere hovels, and most of them like Gurth—the swineherd of Scott's "Ivanhoe"—wearing round their necks the iron collars, which were the badge of Saxon serfdom, and like him driving their herds into the woods each morning, and returning at nightfall with their charges grunting and gorged with beech-mast and acorns.

> While to their lowly dome
> The full-fed swine return'd with evening home;
> Compell'd reluctant, to the several sties,
> With din obstreperous, and ungrateful cries.

The trade and callings of an English serf were as limited as his other opportunities in life; and others beside the swineherd found it in the adjacent woodlands. For there were certainly woodcutters and charcoal burners; and if the local iron ore were exploited, who shall say there were not then Willenhall smiths who fashioned bolts and bars, even if they had not arrived at the intricacies of locks and keys?

Here we are but emerging from the twilight of history.

VII.—A Chapel and a Chantry at Willenhall.

In the earlier centuries of our national existence, the history of a parish follows that of its church, the ecclesiastical fold into which its inhabitants were regularly gathered, not only for every religious purpose, but for every other object of communal interest or of a public nature.

But, as previously explained, Willenhall was not a parish; it was but one member of that wide parochial area ruled from the mother church of Wolverhampton, several miles distant.

Yet at an early period Willenhall seems to have boasted a chapel-of-ease, for the Calendar of Patent Rolls, under date 1297, contains an allusion to "Thomas de Trollesbury, parson of the church of Willenhale." Dr. Oliver, in his history of the town, says that Wolverhampton church was rebuilt about 1342, and he evidently attributes the erection of Willenhall chapel to the same date, as being the outcome of the same devout spirit of church building. But this is nearly half a century later than the allusion just quoted from the Patent Rolls, and Dr. Oliver's reference may possibly be to the founding of a chantry chapel by the Gerveyse family, who set up one of these mass-houses in Willenhall about a dozen years after one had been established at Pelsall.

Let it not be imagined that this new church was either a large or a magnificent structure. In all probability it was a diminutive chapel constructed of timber which had been cut in the adjacent forest; some of its wall spaces, perhaps, were only of timber framed wattle and dab; and at most any building material of a more durable nature entering into its construction would be but a plinth of stone masonry, and dwarfed at that.

A chapel-of-ease, be it explained, was often established where the parish was a wide one, for the "ease" of those parishioners who dwelt at a distance from the mother church, and found it difficult to attend divine service so far away from their homes. Such chapels were intended for prayer and preaching only; burials and administrations of the sacraments being always strictly reserved to the mother church.

While a chapel-of-ease was provided for the general good of the whole community, a chantry chapel was intended for the special glory and exclusive benefit of some local landed family. And here is the first record we have of the Willenhall Chantry; it is extracted from the Patent Rolls of Edward III., under date 14th February, 1328:—

"Licence for the alienation in mortmain by Richard Gerveyse, of Wolvernehampton, of a messuage, land, and a moiety of a mill in Willenhale, co. Stafford, to a Chaplain to celebrate Divine service daily in the Chapel of Willenhale for the souls of the said Richard and Felicia, his wife, the fathers, mothers, brothers, sisters, children and ancestors, and others." A fine of 40s. was paid to the King (at Stafford) for this licence to devote landed estate to the said purposes of church endowment.

A chantry (or chauntry, a name derived from cantaria), was a chapel, little church, or some particular altar in a church, endowed with lands and other revenues, for the maintenance of a priest, or priests, daily to chant a mass and offer prayers for the souls of the donors, and such others as the founders of the chantry may have named. In this particular instance, as we have seen, the eternal welfare of the Gerveyses is sought to be assured, and the chantry here was doubtless at the altar of the new chapel-of-ease—we cannot expect there were two separate ecclesiastical buildings in so small a place as Willenhall.

The method of procedure in setting up these foundations was first to obtain a patent from the Crown for the founding and endowing of them; and then to obtain the Bishop's licence for the regular daily performance of Divine service by the appointed chantry priest, to whose stipend and support the endowment mainly went.

Most of these chantries came into existence in the 14th century, and by the close of the following century there was scarce a parish church in the kingdom without its chantry in one or other of its side chapels or subsidiary altars. By the time of Richard II.—about the year 1394—at least four chantries had been founded, and chapels built, within the outer area of Wolverhampton parish; namely, at Willenhall, Bilston, Pelsall, and Hatherton.

In connection with the endowments of the Willenhall chantry, it is on record that at an Inquisition taken in 1397, it was testified on oath that Roger Levison at that time held on lease from Thomas Browning, chaplain of this chantry, 12 acres of land in Wednesfield, and 100s. of rent in Willenhall, for which he had to perform suit and service (of the usual nature in feudal tenures) at the Deanery Court of Wolverhampton.

In 1409 the advowson of the chapel of Willenhall, together with certain valuable properties of rents and tenements in Wolverhampton, were granted by Richard Hethe and William Prestewode, chaplain, to William Bysshebury and his wife Joan, and settled on them for the term of their lives, with remainder to John Hampton, of Stourton, and his heirs for ever.

Fourteen years later William Bysshebury (his wife Joan being then deceased) was sued by certain plaintiffs, on behalf of the said John Hampton, for wasting these Wolverhampton properties, of which he had the reversion. The plaintiffs included Roger Aston, knight, William Leveson, William Everdon, Thomas Arblaster, and others; while the waste and destruction complained of comprised the digging and selling of clay, marl, and stones; the permitting of seven halls, two chambers, two kitchens, two granges, a dovecot, and a mill to remain unroofed till the principal timbers had rotted; and also with cutting down and selling a number of oaks, ashes, pear, and apple trees, the total damage in respect of all this waste being estimated at a very considerable figure.

The advowson was, of course, the right of presentation to the benefice of Willenhall; and the Hamptons of Stourton Castle, to whom it passed at this time, seem to have been a family which originated at Wolverhampton—and perhaps derived their name from the town.

The ministers who officiated in the local chapels-of-ease were inferior in official status to the vicar, rector, or beneficed clergyman of the mother church, and such curates were generally removable at the pleasure of the said vicar or rector. Willenhall, doubtless, was served by a "curate" sent from the Wolverhampton collegiate establishment.

In the reign of Edward IV. local ecclesiastical matters became further complicated by the collegiate church of Wolverhampton being permanently united with the Deanery of Windsor, the two deaneries being always subsequently held together. It appears that King Edward, desirous of doing his Chaplain a favour, annexed the "Free Royal Church of Wolverhampton" to the said Deanery of Windsor, which royal act was soon afterwards confirmed by Parliament (1480).

The Chantry of Willenhall, in common with all others, disappeared at the Reformation (this one probably in 1545), when prayers for the dead were no longer tolerated. But it is interesting to observe that under the new Protestant régime attendance at church every Sunday was still regarded as a duty no good citizen and loyal subject could be excused.

Attendance at church was compulsory in the early days of the Anglican establishment. By statute (I, Elizabeth c. I., 23 Elizabeth c. I., and 3, James I. c. 4) every person was to repair to his parish church every Sunday on pain of forfeiting 1s. for every offence; and being present at any form of prayer contrary to the Book of Common Prayer was punished with six months' imprisonment. Persons above sixteen years of age who absented themselves from church above a month had to pay a forfeit of £20 a month.

Protestant dissenters who did not deny the doctrine of the Trinity were (it is interesting to note) exempted from these penalties in 1689; and the Roman Catholics were similarly emancipated by law in 1792. This by the way.

It was in Elizabeth's reign, and, of course, under the authority of the newly-established Protestant Church of England, that Willenhall was enabled to make a distinct advance in the status of its church. The charge of this church became an independent one, and was no longer subordinated to the canons of Wolverhampton; the incumbent was thenceforward to be in fact, as well as in name, "Chaplain of Willenhall." But although the incumbent thus obtained his personal freedom from the domination of the mother church, the Wolverhampton establishment still retained all the old parochial rights in the shape of fees and ecclesiastical emoluments. Beyond levying this money tribute, however, the Dean and Rector of Wolverhampton no longer held any control over the internal affairs of the church of St. Giles', in Willenhall. The specified duties of the incumbent of Willenhall (as set forth in a Trust deed of 1603, to which Sir John Leveson is a party) were to conduct Divine service there, and to have his residence within a mile and a half of the church.

VIII.—Willenhall in the Middle Ages.

Having brought the ecclesiastical history of Willenhall up to the enlightened days of Queen Elizabeth, to preserve some sort of chronological arrangement, we leave that section awhile in order to deal with the social life of the place, so far as this may be gleaned from a number of fragmentary sources and isolated references.

The result of these gleanings is naturally very scrappy an disconnected—like the modern periodicals afflicted with the prevalent "snippetitis." Such as they are, however, the local reader may be willing to accept them as being of some little interest.

In the year 1172 the Pipe Rolls, which come next to the Domesday Book among our most ancient national records, and contain a full account of the Crown revenues, return Willenhall, among five other Staffordshire estates, bringing in the sum of £19 7s. 8d. per annum to Henry II. This would represent nowadays a sum twenty times that amount. These estates were Bilston and Rowley Regis, being ancient demesnes of the Crown, and the manors of Leek, Wolstanton, and Penkhull (in the north of the county), which had escheated at the Conquest from the Earl of Mercia. Rowley probably brought in but a few pence at that time, when it formed a part of Clent.

In the same reign (Henry II.) the Canons of Wolverhampton are recorded as holding two hides of land in "Winenhale"—certainly not more than 400 acres in a fertile locality like this.

During the reign of Edward III., his son and heir, the renowned Black Prince, hero of Crecy and Poictiers, claimed (after the manner of those times) the custody and guardianship of Matilda, daughter and heiress of his old comrade in arms, John de Willenhale. The heiress of Willenhall was therefore at this time a royal ward. The earliest holder of this manor who is known by his territorial title seems to be Roger de Wylnale, who (according to Lawley's "History of Bilston," p. 132) was flourishing about the year 1109.

In these earlier centuries of the Middle Ages the machinery the law was crude and ineffective; as a consequence lawlessness was rampant, and everywhere might became right.

The nobles, whenever the weakness of a king emboldened them, fortified their castles, and increased the number of their retainers, whom they reduced to a condition of complete vassalage; and each baron strove to make himself a figure in the great national convulsions which, from time to time, broke out under the malign influences of the feudalism that dominated the whole land and blighted its every hope of progress.

The Franklins, the inferior grade of gentry, who, under the old Saxon system were called Thanes, were often compelled by force of environment to range themselves under the protecting banner of one or other of these petty kings. And where authority was systematically set at defiance by the great and the powerful, inoffensive conduct and dutiful obedience to the laws of the land afforded no guarantee for the security of either life or property.

To these disturbing influences must be added the barbarous severity of the laws of the chase, the vindictive nature of which sometimes made the heavy feudal chains of the common people almost too grievous to be borne. As Willenhall was on the confines of the Royal Forest of Cannock, the oppressive nature of the Forest Laws was not unfelt by the inhabitants of this secluded hamlet.

In 1306, when John de Swynnerton married the daughter and heiress of Philip de Montgomery, Seneschal of the Royal Forest of Cannock, and became Steward of the Forest in customary succession, Willenhall was officially returned, along with a number of surrounding places (Wednesfield, Wednesbury, Darlaston, Essington, Hilton, Newbrigge, Moseley, Bushbury, Pendeford, Coven, and a score more), as appurtenant to a third part of the said forest bailiwick.

The Swynnerton interest in Willenhall transpires again in 1364, when John de Swynnerton is found suing two Willenhall men for forcibly and feloniously removing some of his goods and chattels from that place.

In the previous reign—that of Henry III.—numerous fines for illegal enclosures of Cannock Forest had been imposed upon landowners in this locality. Among them were Stephen de Hulton (or Hilton), and John, his son, "of Wednesfield," who had enclosed with a hedge and a ditch three acres of heath in Wednesfield, which they held under the Dean of Wolverhampton. They were fined four shillings each, and ordered peremptorily to throw down the hedge.

Here is an episode characteristic of the period. It is a Tuesday evening in the month of August, 1347, and about the hour of vespers. The scene is laid in "the field of Wolverhampton, called Wyndefield, in a place called Le Ocstele, near Le More Love-ende." A body of men, all carrying arms, are seen to approach their victim, who is described as a clerk, and therefore presumably defenceless. He is Roger Levessone, son of Richard Levessone. His assailants are Robert le Clerk, of Sedgley, two Dudley men, a man from Bloxwich, and several others, all duly named in the records of the law courts.

What the cause of quarrel may have been these meagre records do not inform us, but on the evidence of a number of witnesses, among whom was Richard Colyns, of Willenhall, they freely used their spears and swords, inflicting wounds upon the throat and other parts of the body, till the unfortunate Roger was despatched.

In 1339, one Richard Adams, of Willenhall, was charged with slaying two men in that place, one a townsman named John Odyes, and a certain John de Bentley. As he was acquitted, probably he did it in self-defence. Encounters of this character were of frequent occurrence in those lawless times.

When the offences recorded are of a less serious nature than murder and slaughter, they are nearly always described as being accompanied by the violent use of lethal weapons—"vi et armis" is the old legal phrase. Here are some examples of this kind of lawlessness:—

In 1352, William de Hampton (probably of the Dunstall family of that name) prosecuted a gang of fourteen men, including a chaplain, the parson of Sheynton (? Shenstone), and two men from Tettenhall, for robbing him of his goods and chattels at Willenhall, Wednesfield, Tettenhall, and Pendeford. Of the details of the robberies we are able to learn nothing, except that they were all perpetrated forcibly, and with a reckless display of violence.

A similar prosecution was undertaken in 1395 by another member of this family, one Nicholas Hampton, against Thomas Marshall, of Willenhall, and for a similar outrage in that place.

A Willenhall man named John Wilson, in 1373, had to invoke the law upon a desperado who forcibly broke into his house and close at Homerwych (Hammerwich), and stole from thence timber, household utensils, clothing, corn, hay, and apparently everything he could lay his hands upon and carry away.

Twenty years later John Wilson (probably the same prosecutor) charged John Wilkes, of Darlaston, with stealing two of his oxen, though no violence is alleged on this occasion.

Two Willenhall men, William Colyns, and William Stokes, were, in 1399, arrested, and charged with cutting down trees and underwood at Bentley. Force and violence were used on that occasion; and it must be remembered that timber was then in much greater demand for building purposes than now, while underwood was in constant requisition as fuel and for the repair of fences and shelters.

Sixteen years later (1415) John Pype and a number of other Bilston men were prosecuted by Sir Hugh Burnell, Knt., for breaking into his closes at Willenhall, trespassing on his land, and treading down his grass with their cattle, committing damage to a grievous extent, and all in undisguised defiance to the law.

Enough has been quoted to illustrate, by incidents common to the social life of so simple a community as that of Willenhall, the gradual decay of feudalism, and the steady growth of English liberty by the vindication of constitutional law.

IX.—The Levesons and other old Willenhall families.

From the same sources, namely from the records of the ancient Law Courts, as transcribed, translated, and published in the volumes of the Salt Society, we are enabled to gain a knowledge of the most prominent families in this locality during the Middle Ages. There seem to have been lawsuits ever since there were landowners.

The principal family in Willenhall were the Levesons or Leusons, who are said to have been connected with this place and the neighbouring parishes of Wednesbury and Wolverhampton, almost from the time of the Norman Conquest, eking out a living from the soil, of which their tenure was at first a very precarious one.

Their pedigree, given by the county historian, Shaw (II. p. 169), shows the founder to be one Richard Leveson, settled in Willenhall in the reign of Edward I. But we find that in the year before this king's accession, namely, in 1271, Richard Levison paid a fine of 2s. 3d. in the Forest Court for being permitted to retain in cultivation an assart of half an acre, lying in Willenhall; that is, to be allowed to continue under the plough a piece of land on which he had grubbed up all the trees and bushes by the roots, to the detriment of the covert within the King's Royal Forest of Cannock.

The founder of the family was succeeded by a son, and by a grandson, both of whom were also called "Richard Leveson, of Willenhall," although the last one was sometimes designated as "of Wolverhampton," to which town he was doubtless attracted by the greater profits to be made in the wool trade.

The early commercial fame of Wolverhampton was based on this industry. Although there were no wool-staplers here in 1340, yet in 1354, when the wool staple was removed from Flanders, Wolverhampton was one of the few English towns fixed upon by Parliament for carrying on the trade. (A staple, it may be explained, is a public mart appointed and regulated by law.) Although the staple was again changed to Calais, it was speedily brought back to England, and the Levesons were soon among the foremost "merchants of the staple."

A Clement de Willenhale is mentioned in an Assize of the year 1338, but not improbably he was identical with the Clement Leveson mentioned in another lawsuit in 1356, a party to which was a member of the ancient local family of Harper—"John le Harpere," as he is therein called.

Then there is mention in 1351 of the John de Willenhale, who is described as being in the wardship of the Prince of Wales. But perhaps the best insight into the social state of Willenhall at this period will be obtained from a consideration of its inhabitants liable to pay a war tax which was levied by

Edward III. in order to enable him to carry on a war of defence against Scotland. For this popular military expedition, Parliament in 1327 granted the youthful king a Subsidy to the amount of one-twentieth leviable upon the value of nearly all kinds of property. Assessors and collectors were appointed for every town and village, and they were sworn to make true returns of every man's goods and chattels, both in the house and out of it. The exceptions allowable were the goods of those whose total property did not amount to the full value of ten shillings; the tools of trade; and the implements of agriculture. On the face of it, these exemptions seem fair and just to the lower orders; but we find the higher orders were also favoured, and unduly so; not so much perhaps in the matters of armour and cavalry horses, as in the non-liability of the robes and jewels of knights, gentlemen, and their wives, as well as of their silver and household plate.

Here is a copy of the Subsidy Roll of 1327 so far as it relates to

WYLLUNHALE.

De	s.	d.
Adam M—	—	—
Andr' atte Mere		xviij
Joh'e le Bakere	—	—
Ric'o Odys	ij	
Ric'o filio Radulfi	ij	vj
Joh'e filio Rogeri	—	—
Ric'o filio Ade	ij	
Will'o filio Roberti	iij	
Will'o atte Pirye	vj	
Ric'o Chollettes	ij	
Agnete Odys	iij	
Hugone le Gardiner		ij
Adame atte Mere	ij	
Joh'e Hopkynes		xij
Agnete atte Wode		xij

Will'mo Newemon		xij
Symone Levesone		vj
Summa	xxviij	vj Pb.

It will be seen that this fragment is imperfect, as the various amounts set down will not add up to the "summa" or total given, notwithstanding that it has been audited—the abbreviation "Pb." standing for probata, or proved.

But more interest will be found in a brief study of the names of Willenhall's inhabitants, who were men of substance seven hundred years ago.

It will be observed that Simon is the only member of the Leveson family assessed, and that he pays the least sum, except that paid by the man Hugh, described as "the Gardener" (the amount paid by "John the Baker" has been obliterated from the roll).

The strange surname Odyes, appearing twice in this list, occurs in another record of the year 1422, and seems to belong to a gentle family, resident in Willenhall, and owning lands in Bentley.

As but few people then bore recognised surnames, we find taxpayers here officially set down as "Richard the son of Ralph," "John the son of Roger," "Richard the son of Adam," and "William the son of Robert." Besides these named according to their parentage, we have those described according to their place of residence; as thus, "Andrew at the Mere," and "Adam at the Mere"; "Agnes at the Wood," and "William at the Pear Tree." William Newman was probably so-called because he was a new-comer, or was lately emancipated from serfdom as a "new man."

From the Patent Rolls of November, 1334, may be gleaned the bare facts of what seems to have been an extraordinary assault at Willenhall, which was committed upon John, son of John de Bentley, by no less than thirty assailants. Among those implicated may be noted the names of five members of the Leveson family, namely, Geoffrey, Moses, John, Simon, and Simon the younger; also the names of William, son of Robert atte Pirie, Andrew atte Mere, John le Harpere, Richard Coletes, Richard Colyns, and several others which have occurred before in these pages. The Leveson family continue to make many appearances in the records of Willenhall litigation at this early period. In 1347, Andrew, the son of Simon Levesone, of Willenhale, was sued for the treading down and consuming of the corn of Andrew in le Lone at Willenhale, with his cattle, and by force of arms, and for cutting down his trees, and beating and wounding his servant.

In the following year, Geoffrey Levesone, of Willenhale, brought a somewhat similar charge of trespass against John Oldejones, of Wodnesfeld. In 1362,

Roger Levesone, of Willenhale, was successful in a suit for recovering two acres of land at Wolverhampton. About the same time Juliana Levesone, of Willenhall, married William Tomkys, a member of one of the leading families of Bilston.

In 1369, John de la Lone, of Wolverhampton, sued John Levesone, of Willenhale, for forcibly taking his fish, to the value of 100 shillings, "from his several fishery in Willenhale."

In 1394, Roger Liefson (Leveson), of Wylenhale (who has been previously mentioned in Chapter VII.), was at law with Thomas Colyns, of the same place, for forcibly taking away from Willenhall twelve oxen belonging to him. Immediately after, one William de Chorley was attacked for taking away from Great Wyrley, also with a display of armed force, three oxen and two cows, the property of Richard Leveson, of Willenhall. If these two cases were not reprisals, they at least show a state of disturbance and insecurity.

Another exhibition of lawlessness is brought to our notice in 1429, when Richard Leveson is found suing Robert Dorlaston, weaver, Richard Colyns, lorymer, William Brugge, and William Bate, yeomen, all described as "of Wylenhale," for violently and forcibly breaking into his close at Willenhall.

A similar case of forcible entry into the close and houses of James Leveson, at Willenhale, by one Roger Waters, a Willenhale lorymer, was an outrage which occupied the attention of the law courts in 1433.

Three years later (1436) another law case shows the same James Levesson suing John Pippard, chaplain, for a messuage and 20 acres of land in Wolverhampton, which he asserted had descended to him from Richard Levesson, of Willenhall, who held it in the time of Edward I., in a direct line, namely, from Richard to his son Geoffrey, from Geoffrey to his son Roger, and from Roger to his son Nicholas, who was plaintiff's father.

By this time the Leveson family seems to have been not only firmly established in and around Willenhall, Wednesfield, and Wolverhampton, but to have been very numerous as well. Originally yeomen of the first-named place, cultivating their lands within the precincts of the Royal Forest of Cannock, they gradually grew and prospered, one branch taking advantage of the greater commercial opportunities offered by the last-named town, and settling there as merchants and wool-staplers.

Woolstapling was a prosperous trade in Wolverhampton as early as 1354; and in its ancient market place the Levesons of the younger branch were to be found bartering wool and steadily accumulating riches until they were able to marry into the most exclusive of the county families.

Among the Bailiffs of the Staple—which, in the case of Wolverhampton were wool and woolfel—we find the names of William Leveson in 1485, and Walter Leveson in 1491.

Members of other old and well-known local families also filled this office of Bailiff at various times, namely, William Jennings in 1483, Richard Gough in 1486, Edward Giffard in 1493, Y. Turton in 1496, and W. Wrottesley in 1499. If evidence were required of the enterprise of these Wolverhampton merchants, it would be forthcoming in the fact that a Leveson and a Jennings, both natives of this place (the latter a "merchant taylor" in 1508) filled the high office of Lord Mayor of London.

An Inquisition Post Mortem (one of those feudal inquiries into the extent of a man's landed possessions which passed to his heirs) was held on the death of Henry Beaumont, lord of the Manor of Wednesbury, at Willenhall, on 28th June, 1472. Among those sworn of the jury on that occasion were James Leveson Esq., Richard Leveson, Esq., Cornelius Wyrley, Esq., Robert Leveson, Ralph Busshbury, Esq., and William Mollesley, all local magnates.

It has not been possible to identify all the members of this extensive family. There were two distinct branches of the Levesons or Luesons. The elder line were of Prestwood and Lilleshall, and produced Sir Richard Leveson, of Trentham; the younger branch, descended from William, the son of Richard Leveson, of Willenhall, produced the Sir Thomas Leveson who was the Royalist governor of Dudley Castle during the great Civil War (1643).

The elder line were "of Prestwood" because Nicholas Leveson, in the time of Henry VI. married Maud, heiress of John de Prestwood. The Lilleshall and other properties were fat church lands, purchased by the wealthy Levesons at the Dissolution of the Monasteries. It was a Richard Leveson of the Prestwood branch who acquired the Haling Estate in Kent by marriage with a Lord Mayor's daughter, and died in 1539 after being himself Lord Mayor of London.

Also from this branch came the famous Vice-Admiral of England in Queen Elizabeth's days. This gallant sea-dog, whose romance with the "Spanish Lady" has been retold by the present writer in his "Staffordshire Stories" (pp. 22–35), took part in that daring attack upon Cadiz which has been sung by Henry John Newbolt in his "Admirals All"—

> Essex was fretting in Cadiz Bay
>   With the galleons fair in sight;
> Howard at last must give him his way,
>   And the word was passed to fight.
> Never was schoolboy gayer than he,
>   Since holidays first began:

> He tossed his bonnet to wind and sea,
> And under the guns he ran.

Admiral Leveson's effigy in Wolverhampton Church stamps him as one of the heroes of old romance—his career was indeed remarkable, as may be read in the work alluded to.

The present-day representatives of the family are the Leveson-Gowers, the head of whom is the Duke of Sutherland. The Gowers were an Anglo-Saxon family seated in Yorkshire, and the union of the two occurred about the time of Charles I., when Sir Thomas Gower, then Sheriff of Yorkshire, married Frances, daughter and co-heir of Sir John Leveson, of Haling and Lilleshall.

At the time Richard Leveson was sailing the seas with Essex and Drake, there was a John Leveson living in Willenhall as lord of the manor, the site of his residence being still marked by the position of Levison Street and Moat Street.

In Wolverhampton "Turton's Old Hall" was originally known as Leveson's Hall; this massive old mansion, surrounded by its once deep and wide moat, is believed to have been erected by John Leveson, a wool merchant, who was High Sheriff of Staffordshire in 1561.

Truly the local record of the Levesons is a long and notable one; and it is interesting to note that John Leveson, son of Thomas, who had been Sheriff of the county, and died in 1595, is the last in Shaw's pedigree to be described as "of Willenhale," although in a succeeding chapter we shall find members of this family still seated on their native soil, Willenhall, as late as the years of the Jacobite Rebellions, 1715 and 1745.

X.—Willenhall Endowments at the Reformation.

Now to resume the ecclesiastical history of the place. Willenhall was affected by the Reformation from two directions; first, through the mother church of Wolverhampton, of which collegiate establishment it formed a portion; secondly, through its own chapel and the endowed chantry established therein.

The great ecclesiastical upheaval of the sixteenth century had its precursor in the Dissolution of the Monasteries by Henry VIII. The rumble of the coming storm warned the secular or non-monastic foundations that it would be prudent to set their houses in order if they were to safeguard their revenues; for every one of the smaller monasteries, with an income of less than £200 per annum, had been forfeited to the Crown (1529).

A new valuation of the College of Wolverhampton had but just been instituted in 1526, from which it will be necessary here to extract only that portion of the return relating to our subject. It was to this effect:—

The Prebend of Wylnall.			
	£	s.	d.
William Leveson, Clerk (dwelling in Exeter with the Bishop), Prebendary there, and hath in glebe-lands	3	0	0
And in tithes of corn, one year with another	3	0	0
And in wool and lambs by the year, one year with another	3	6	8
And in the Easter Book by the year, one year with another	0	13	4
And in tithes of Herbage, Pigs, Geese, and other small tithes	0	40	0
Sum total	12	0	0
And thereof he pays allowance for Synodals every third year, paid to the aforesaid Dean	0	6	8
And so there remains clear	11	13	4
The tenth part thereof	0	23	4

The value of the Deanery, the Prebends, and the two Chantries of Willenhall and Bilston are all set forth in this Return. (See Oliver's "History of Wolverhampton Church," pp. 57–60.)

The visitation of the religious houses, undertaken as it was in a hostile spirit by Henry VIII., naturally alarmed the authorities of a church where it would appear that irregularities on the part of the prebendaries had long existed, and not an inconsiderable portion of the church property had been alienated, to say nothing of the sequestration of the church communion plate. Now some hasty attempts were made at restitution, and more so to escape detection and censure.

Restoration in some sort seems to have been hastily attempted at Wolverhampton. In 1529 Nicholas Leveson presented a new chalice of silver; and the high altar was restored at much expense to its former magnificence. The Dean, however, fell into disgrace in the matter of denying the King's supremacy, and was committed to the Tower of London in consequence. In 1540 bells purchased by the inhabitants from Wenlock Abbey were hung in the church tower. Four years later sixteen stalls, taken from the recently dissolved monastery at Lilleshall, were presented by Sir Walter Leveson to Wolverhampton Church.

All these precautions scarcely availed to avert the impending doom. By an Act passed in the first year of the reign of Edward VI., the dissolution of Colleges and Chantries was effected. But the Royal College of Windsor, of which Wolverhampton was a member, was especially exempted, and the Wolverhampton Chapter consequently felt secure from disturbance.

So sure of their position were they that the prebendaries actually proceeded to lease out their property. Among the others, the prebendary of Willenhall granted his lands and tithes to John Leveson, Esq. (who held several other of the prebendal properties), for a reserved rent of £6 6s.

Although the various deeds were confirmed by the Dean and Chapter of Windsor, the legality of the proceedings was questioned; and presently it was successfully contended that the Deanery of Wolverhampton was a separate benefice detached from the College of Windsor, and that the prebends were in the hands of the Crown.

There is extant another valuation of these ecclesiastical revenues in the Primate's Court. The record is in Latin, but it may be Englished thus:—

	£	s.	d.
Canterbury values Willenhall	5	2	1
It Days to the Dean of Wolverhampton (William Leveson, Prebendary of Willenhall.)	0	3	3

The Prebendary of Willenhall is worth per annum:—

	s.	d.
In Glebeland	41	0
In Corn tithes	40	0
In Wool and Lambs	46	8
In Easter dues	13	10
In Tithes of Fodder, of Hogs, and Geese and other small tithes	40	0
Thence is paid, in every third year, to the Dean, for the Synod	6	8

The valuation of Wolverhampton College which is to be regarded as that of the Reformation was made in 1551, and one item in which may be quoted from Oliver's "History of Wolverhampton Church" (p. 63):—"And for £12 6s. 8d. for the farm of the Prebend of Willnall, with all messuages, tithes, lands, rents, services, and other profits to the said Prebend belonging, demised to John Horton, by Indenture under seal of the said College, dated 4th November, 33 Henry VIII., for the term of 21 years," &c., &c.

Turning our attention to Willenhall itself, let us see how the Chapel here was affected. The Chantry foundation of this Chapel, like all others, had to go. Chantries being founded by the pious rich to have the souls of their dear departed prayed for, could not be tolerated by the Protestant reformers, and were all rigidly suppressed. Here is the valuation formally taken in the reign of Henry VIII. (1526), as before mentioned:—

CHANTRY OF WYLNALL.		
Hugh Bromehall, chaplain, hath a house with lands pertaining to the same, value per annum	8 marks	
	s.	d.
And prays to be allowed for rents of assize, payable to the Dean	3	3
And for Capitation rents, paid annually to William Leveson, Prebendary of Wylnall		10
And so their remains due	102	7
The tenth part thereof	10	3

The Chantry, being regarded as one of the abhorred institutions of Romanism, thus came to an end under the reforming zeal of our Protestant legislators in the early years of the reign of Edward VI.

All the possessions of the Colleges of Wolverhampton and Tettenhall, with their Prebends, together with the Chantry lands of Willenhall, Bilston, and Kinver, when they passed from the Crown in 1552, fell into the hands of the notorious John Dudley, Duke of Northumberland, who contrived to grab no end of church property in this immediate locality. When Northumberland came to the block shortly afterwards, there was a great redistribution of this property, that of Wolverhampton being once more annexed to the Royal Free Chapel of St. George at Windsor.

XI.—How the Reformation Affected Willenhall.

As recorded in the last chapter, the Willenhall Chantry, in common with all others throughout the country, was finally suppressed by Edward VI. and his Protestant ministers (1547). It had been in existence upwards of 200 years, the name of its first Chantry Priest being given (1341) as "William in the Lone."

The Prebendal lands also, as we have seen, were leased in the fourth year of this reign to John Leveson, for the sum of £6 6s. per annum. All the other lands belonging to the Deanery of Wolverhampton then passed into the hands of the King, but did not long remain in the Crown, being conveyed, with much more ecclesiastical property hereabouts, to John Dudley, Duke of Northumberland. On his attainder in the reign of Mary (1553), the Deanery lands reverted to the Crown, to be again restored to their original use by that most pious queen.

In 1547 the zeal of the Protestant reformers induced the Government of Edward VI. to send Commissioners round the country to make inquiry in every parish and every church as to the ecclesiastical appointments used in ritual, with orders to suppress all that made for "idolatrous Popish practices."

The Commissioners for this locality were all men of high standing in the county, as will be seen from their names. They were sworn to make—

> A juste, treu, and parfett survey and inventorie of all goods, plate, juelles, vestements, belles, and other ornaments, of all churches, chappells, brotherhoddes, gyldes, fraternities, and compones within the Hundred of Offeley, in the Countie of Stafford; taken the seventh day of October, in the sixte yere of the Rayne of our Sovereyn Lord, King Edward the Sixte, by Thomas Gyffard and Thomas Fytzherbert, knyghts; and Walter Wrottesley, Esquier, by virtue of the King's commissein to them, directed in that behalf, as hereafter particularly appereth.

On one hand, they had to put a stop to the embezzlement, concealment, and appropriation by private persons of the condemned church property, and to recover as much of it as possible for the King's Exchequer. For, under pretence of a burning zeal for the reformed faith, there had been much sacrilegious spoliation—church plate finding its way on to the table of the neighbouring gentry, marble coffins being utilised as horse-troughs, altar cloths serving as tapestry for parlour walls, and similar malpractices by those who ought to have known better. This property was to be retrieved, and the detected offenders were to be heavily fined.

The Return made for Willenhall Church by the Commissioners and their official "Surveyor," or assessor, runs, verbatim:—

> WYLNALL.
>
> Fyrste one challes of sylver with a paten parcell gilte weyinge by estimacon viij ounces; iij vestement one of whyte fustian another of blacke chamlett and the thyrd of bleu sarsynet; iij alter clothes; ij cruetts of ledde; a bucket of brasse; iij candelstyks of maslyn; a paxe of brass; a corporas with the case; ij towells; one cheste; a lampe of latynn; ij small bells.
>
> Mem.—That all these parcells before rekened were delyvered unto Richard Forsett, Surveyor to the Kynge's Majesti, as shall appare by his acquytance, except ij belles the whyche remayne still within the sayd chapell.

A few words in explanation of the above terms may, perhaps, be necessary for the general reader. The chalice and the paten were the vessels used at the Sacrament, the former being the wine cup, which was of silver, and the latter the bread dish, partly gilt. The priestly vestments were those forbidden by the reformed church, and were of different textures for different parts of the Roman ceremonial; the fustian was a coarse piled fabric, or kind of cotton velvet, imported from the East; chamlett, or camlett, was a cloth so called because originally woven from camel hair; and the sarsnett was a thin kind of silk. The altar cloths had to be discarded when the "Mass" was reformed into the "Holy Communion." The cruets were pairs of metal jars for containing the wine and the water previous to their admixture in the sacrament of the Mass. The bucket was for use at the font. The candlesticks were for the lighted tapers upon the altar and in this case were made of maslin, an alloy like brass, but with a harder grain; latten, of which the altar lamp was made, was a similar alloy resembling brass. The pax was a tablet (sometimes of wood, sometimes of bread, though this Willenhall example was of durable brass), on which was a figure of the crucifixion; it was presented in the ceremony of the Mass for the faithful to kiss. The Corporas was the cloth placed beneath the consecrated elements in the service of the Mass. The towels were napkins used in the celebration of the sacred office; it must be borne in mind that all textile fabrics, as well as metals, were far more costly in those days, and the chest was to keep all these valuables in safety.

It is difficult to decide the nature of the "two small bells"; because, if they were the sanctus bells used at the most solemn parts in the performance of the Mass, one a hand-bell rung inside, and the other as a signal outside, they would have been abolished. So, as they were left by the Reformers, they were probably small bells in the steeple or turret.

So much for the changes materialistic brought about at this great religious upheaval of the sixteenth century. Now let us inquire into the more serious and essential changes which occurred in the religious life of the nation at that time.

From a little known Return made in 1586 we are enabled to gather the conditions of the Church of England, as it was found to exist, only 28 years after it had been by law established.

At the Reformation, after the annulling of all "Popish ordinations," the state of the English clergy became very deplorable. Some of the basest of the people were permitted to become parish priests, a circumstance that gave point to the arguments and contentions of the Puritans.

The Reformers were divided upon the subject, Queen Elizabeth expressing herself as being perfectly satisfied if in each county three or four clergymen could be found capable of preaching to their congregations. The Puritans, on the other hand, laid great stress on the admonitory value and spiritual importance of sermons and homilies.

By 1586 the condition of the newly-formed Protestant Church of England had become so scandalous in respect of its priesthood that a national "Survey" was undertaken. Of the remarkable facts disclosed by this Return we select from the summaries the following few which relate to this immediate locality:—

> WOLVERHAMPTON.—A Collegiate Church; impropriate to the King's Majestie or the Dean of Windsor; value of lands belonging to it is £600 per annum. There be seven Prebends and a Sexton under them; seven stipendiaries; the allowance for four of them is ten nobles apiece; for the other three £6 apiece. Six of the Prebends be held by Sir Gualter Levison; the other is held by another. The rent reserved to the Dean of Windsor, £38. People 4,000. Many Popish; many Recusants.
>
> Chappells 3:—
>
> 1. Pelsall; curate's stipend £4; no preacher.
>
> 2. Willenhall; curate hath no stipend reserved; no preacher.
>
> 3. Bilston; curate hath no stipend reserved; no preacher.
>
> These curates, especially two of them, Mounsell and Cooper, be notorious and dissolute men.

Such was the lamentable state of the local clergy at that time, when the population of Wolverhampton, with all its outlying parts, is set down at 4,000 only. A few words of explanation will perhaps be necessary to make the foregoing extract more intelligible to the general reader.

A "noble" was a coin of the value of 6s. 8d.; a "recusant" was one who disputed the authority and supremacy of the Crown in matters ecclesiastical, whether Papist or Puritan; while to "impropriate" church property was to place it in the hands of a layman.

Four or five more extracts from this interesting Survey, relating to other parts of this neighbourhood, may not be out of place to quote here:—

> BYSHBY.—Parsonage, impropriate; worth £40 per annum; vicarage worth £30; patron, Sir Edward Littleton; many Popish; many Recusants. Incumbent a mere worldling; no preacher.
>
> TETNALL.—A college dissolved; five prebends and a deane; impropriate to the King's Majestie; worth 300 marks. One prebend is held by Sir Richard Leveson; one by Mr. Gualter Wriotesley; two by Richard Cresswell. Curate's stipend, 20 marks; no preacher.
>
> CODSALL.—Prebend of Tetnall. Curate-prebendary a loose liver; no preacher.
>
> WOMBOURNE.—Parsonage, impropriate, held by Hugh Wriotesley, Esquire; worth £40; vicarage worth £26; patron, Edward L. Dudley.
>
> PEN.—Parsonage; impropriate to the vicars of Lichfield; worth £20; vicarage worth as much; patrons, the Vicars of Lichfield. Vicar —; no preacher.

This selection of extracts will serve to enlighten the reader upon two important points in the history of the Church; the first is the amount of church revenue which had already found its way into the pockets of the laity; and the other is the lamentable necessity there was at that period to provide the English clergy with ready-made Homilies. These Homilies were ordered (as the Prayer Book informs us, in the XXXV. Article), to be read "diligently and distinctly" in the churches by the Ministers.

XII.—Before the Reformation—and After.

It may be assumed that Willenhall Church has been dedicated to St. Giles from the first, because the period for holding the dedicatory Wake synchronises with St. Gile's day (September 1st), making allowance for the eleven days' difference effected in 1752 between the Old Style and the New Style calendars. As the Protestant Reformers took objection to non-Biblical saints (West Bromwich Church was altered from St. Clement's to All Saints'), a dedication to St. Giles may safely be accepted as a pre-Reformation one; and as St. Giles was the patron saint of cripples, he doubtless retained his popularity here on account of the reputation for healing qualities acquired by the Willenhall "Holy Well"—of which more anon. But in addition to its Wake, the town seems to have possessed in mediæval times a much frequented Summer Fair, held on Trinity Sunday. Our knowledge of this interesting fact is derived from the records of the Court of Star Chamber.

This court was established by Henry VII. to deal with routs, riots, and all other cases not sufficiently provided for by the common law; but the oppression practised by the unscrupulous abuse of its indefinite jurisdiction led to its summary extinction in the reign of Charles I.

The case to be quoted is one of an alleged riot in the year 1498 (13 Henry VII.), in which the men of Wednesbury were deeply involved. These turbulent townsmen seem to have made themselves notorious for riotous behaviour at various times; as witness the historic Wesley Riots of 1744, their march on Birmingham to regulate the price of malt in 1782, and their attack on the same town during the Church and King Riots in 1791.

It would appear that a company of Mummers, made up of performers from Wolverhampton, Wednesbury, and Walsall, were regularly in the habit of going round to the neighbouring Fairs, and performing to the accompaniment of pipe and tabor a Morris-dance, in which the characters were dressed up for the then popular dramatic interlude of "Robin Hood," including Maid Marian, Friar Tuck, and all the rest of them.

>The hobby-horse doth hither prance,
>Maid Marian and the Morris-dance.

It would be interesting to discover why, in this local version, the character called the "Abbot of Marham" was introduced into the play—Marham nunnery was situated in Norfolk, a long way from the usual forest scenes of Sherwood and Needwood.

The money collected at these al fresco performances was applied to maintaining the fabric of the three parish churches; but, for some reason unknown, there had evidently grown up a deadly feud between the

Wednesbury and the Walsall contingents. This was the cause of all the trouble.

The "John Beamont" mentioned was John Beaumont, Esquire, lord of the manor of Wednesbury, a benefactor of the parish church there, and a patron of a Walsall Chantry. It will be noticed that the quoted document speaks of the "Church of the lordship," not "of the parish"; and also, that the prefix "Sir" was then used to a parson's name, as we should now use the prefix "Rev."

Here is the text of the plaints entered by the terrorised "orators" of Walsall, together with the affidavits put in as rejoinders; the archaic spelling is retained only in a few places just to indicate the style of English then employed in the law courts; and it is interesting to note that Midlanders had those peculiar vowel sounds in olden times, and pronounced "fetch" as "fatch," and "gather" as "gether"—just as the illiterate among them still do:—

> TO THE KING OUR SOVEREIGN LORD—
>
> Humbly sheweth unto your highness, your faithful subject and true liegeman, Roger Dyngley, Mayor of Walsall; and Thomas Rice, of the same town—That whereas your said orators on Wednesday next before Trinity Sunday, the 13th year of your reign, were in God's peace and yours, in your said town of Walsall—thither came one John Cradeley, of Wednesbury, and Thomas Morres, of Dudley, in your said county; and then and there made affray upon the said Thomas Rice, "and hym soore wounded and bett" [beat], so that he was in peril of his life.
>
> Whereupon the said Mayor, with other inhabitants, did arrest John Cradeley and Thomas Morres, and there did put them in prison according to your laws, there to remain till it were known whether the said Thomas Rice should live or die.
>
> And incontinent thereupon one John Beamonde, "Squyer," Walter Levison, of Wolverhampton, Richard Foxe, priest, of the same town, and one Robert Marshall, of Wednesbury, "arreysed" and riotously assembled themselves at Wednesbury with other riotous persons to the number of 200 men, arrayed in manner of war, that is to say, with bows, arrows, bills, and "gleves" [long daggers], with other unlawful weapons there gathered and assembled, to the intent to have come to have destroyed your said town of Walsall, saying openly that they would "fache" out of

prison the said John Cradeley and Thomas Morres, and destroy your said town of Walsall.

And thereupon William Harper and William Wilkes, Justices of the Peace, charged the said riotous persons to keep the peace upon a great pain to be forfeited to your grace. By reason whereof the said rioters for that time ceased from further riot.

And whereas the said Justices of the Peace, knowing the said rioters intended to make more riot, and to execute their malice in doing some mischief or hurt to the said town or to the inhabitants thereof, for eschewing any riot or breach of the peace commanded the inhabitants of Walsall, Wednesbury, and of divers other towns, their adherents, that they should not assemble together out of the said town, and should not come to a Fair that should be holden at Wilnale on Trinity Sunday, then next following.

And the inhabitants of Walsall the same day kept at home.

Notwithstanding, came one from Hampton, whose name is William Milner, calling himself the Abbot of Marram, and one Walter Leveson with him, with the inhabitants of Hampton to the number of four score persons in harness [armour] after the manner of war, to Wilnall to the said Fair. And also one Robert Marchall, of Wednesbury, calling himself Robyn Hood, and Sir Richard Foxe, priest, with divers other persons to the number of 100 men and above, in harness, came in likewise, and met with the said other rioters at the said town of Wilnall, and then and there riotously assembled themselves, commanding openly that if any of the town of Walsall came therefrom, to strike them down, and in the said town continued their said riotous assembly all the same day; and if any man of Walsall at that day had been seen at that Fair, they should have been in jeopardy of their lives.

Please your highness to grant your Letters of Privy Seal to be directed to the said John Beamonde, Walter Leveson, Sir Richard Foxe, priest, and Roger Marchall, to commanding them to appear before your Council to answer to the premises.

1st July, in the 13th year, to appear.

[Endorsed].

Three several letters issued to Walter Leveson, Richard Foxe, and Roger Marchall, to appear.

> MICHAELMAS TERM IN THE 14TH YEAR. THE MAYOR AND INHABITANTS OF WALSALL AGAINST JOHN BEAMONDE, ESQUIRE, AND OTHERS. ANSWER FOR SIR ROGER MARCHALL—

The Bill is only "feyned a yenst hym in pure males" [malice] for his great trouble and vexation, and loss of his goods. He did not riotously assemble with any persons in arms, nor is he guilty of any riot. As for the coming to the said Fair at Wylnahale "hit hath byn of olde tymes used and accustumed in the said Fere day that with the inhabitants of sede townes of Hampton, Wednesbury, and Walsall have comyne to the said Fere with the capitanns called the Abot of Marham or Robyn Hodys, to the intent to gether money with their disportes to the profight of the chirches of the said lordshipes," whereby great profit hath grown to the said churches in times past.

Whereupon the said Roger Marchall and his Company at the special desire of the Inhabitants of Weddesbury, come in peaceable manner to the said Fair, according to the said old custom, and these met with one John Walker, of Walsall, and divers others of the said town, and then and there "they make as gud chere unto them as they should do to ther lovying neyburs." And he denies that they came riotously.

THE ANSWER OF WALTER LEVESON—

He heard say at Hampton, where he dwells, that a "rumour and mysdemenying" against the King's peace was had in Walsale, and that the inhabitants were riotously disposed against John Beamont.

Whereupon the said Walter with two of his servants, in peaceable manner, and without any harness, came to the said John Beamont to his place at Weddesbury, to know how the Mayor and Inhabitants of Walsale would entreat him.

John Beamont said that he knew of no hurt that they willed to him. It has been of old time used and accustomed on the said Fair day that the inhabitants of Hampton, Weddesbury, and Walsale have come to the Fair with such

Captains as they have of old time used, to the intent to gather money with their disports to the use of the said churches of the said lordships.

And this is all we know of that lively "Whitsun Morris" at Willenhall Fair in the year of grace 1498. It all reads like a delightful chapter in the vein of Shakespeare's Dogberry and Verges; and it will be noted that the priests are among the captains or ringleaders in this Sunday revelling.

* * * * *

After the Reformation came the Puritans, who severely discountenanced all Sunday revelry. And so the lampoon of their enemies ran:—

> There dwells a people on the earth
> That reckons true religion treason,
> That makes sad war on holy mirth,
> Count madness zeal and nonsense reason;
> That think no freedom but in slavery,
> That makes lyes truth, religion, knavery;
> That rob and cheat with "yea" and "nay,"
> Riddle me, riddle me, who are they?

Yet, when religious differences had brought on civil war, it had to be confessed of this Puritan people (so says Sir Francis Doyle in "The Cavalier"):—

> That though they snuffled psalms, to give
>   The rebel dogs their due,
> When the roaring shot poured thick and hot
>   They were stalwart men and true.

And so the mighty struggle for liberty of conscience against the pretensions of a dominant Church had proceeded for over century, when we find the incumbency of Willenhall held by the Rev. Thomas Badland.

Thomas Badland was born in 1643, matriculated at Pembroke College, Oxford, 1650, and took his B.A. degree, 1653. He was one of the noble band of ministers who relinquished their livings on August 24th, 1662, rather than conform to the requirements of the Act of Uniformity, passed on the Restoration of Charles II.

On his ejectment from Willenhall, this conscientious Puritan divine returned to his native city, Worcester, where "he formed a distinct congregation of Christians, who assembled for worship in a small room" at the bottom of Fish Street. His family was an old one in Worcester, the name Badland occurring in a charter of James I.

According to Noake's "Worcester Sects," he was minister of that congregation for 35 years; but before his death the Declaration of Indulgence by James II. was made (1687), and immediately thereupon Mr. Badland's church was regularly constituted by the adoption of the Covenants of church membership which had been drawn by Richard Baxter—he was a personal friend of the eminent divine—in terms sufficiently general to include almost all denominations who might choose to make it a point of common agreement.

From Nash's "History of Worcestershire" we learn that on a monument on the south wall of the south aisle of St. Martin's church, Worcester, it was set forth:—

> Under these seats lies interred the body of the Rev. Thomas Badland, a faithful and profitable preacher of the Gospel in this city for the space of thirty-five years. He rested from his labours, May 5th, A.D 1698, æt. 64.
>
> Mors mihi vita nova.

When St. Martin's Church was pulled down in 1768 this marble tablet was carelessly thrown aside, and soon got broken into fragments. Happily the pieces were rescued and put together again with loving care for erection in the vestibule of Angel Street Chapel, at the expense of the congregation worshipping there. In the new Independent Chapel, which has taken the place of that older building (registered at Quarter Sessions in 1689 as a Presbyterian place of worship), the memorial has been placed near the pulpit.

From a MS. history of Angel Street Church, written by Samuel Blackwell in 1841, it would appear that Mr. Badland had as one of his assistants a Mr. Hand, who had been ordained at Oldbury. At Fish Street Chapel (the site of which was occupied in later times by Dent's Glove Factory), there were 120 Communicants in February, 1687; and the Declaration of Faith drawn up and signed by the church members that year bears first the name of Thomas Badland, pastor, and among many others that follow is that of "Elizab. Badland," presumably his wife. Such, briefly, is the life history of the good man who relinquished the living of Willenhall, and repudiated its "idolatrous steeple-house," at the Black Bartholomew of 1662, rather than stifle the dictates of his conscience.

In Palmer's "Nonconformist' Memorials" the Rev. Thomas Badland has been confused with the Rev. Thomas Baldwin, who was ejected (1662) from the Vicarage of Chaddesley Corbett, and who died at Kidderminster in 1693, his funeral sermon being preached by a conforming clergyman there, named White. There was also a Thomas Baldwin, junior, who had been expelled from the Vicarage of Clent, and died at Birmingham; but notwithstanding such common mispronunciations as "Badlam" for "Badland," it seems clear that the facts of the Rev. Mr. Badland's life are as given here, thanks to the careful researches of Mr. A. A. Rollason, of Dudley.

XIII.—A Century of Wars, Incursions, and Alarms (1640–1745).

Life in Willenhall, as in many other places during the Stuart period, was not without its alarms and apprehensions. The trouble began when Charles I., by the advice of Archbishop Laud, tried to force the English liturgy upon Scotland. The resistance offered to this was the real beginning of the English Revolution, for the King, in the attempt to carry out his despotic will, had to enlist soldiers by force.

In the year 1640 a special muster was made for the war against the Scotch Covenanters; the men from Staffordshire consisted of trained bands who had been employed in the previous year, and 300 men who were impressed for the occasion. The service throughout the country was very unpopular, and in some counties the men mutinied and murdered their officers. Staffordshire did not escape some riots, and one of the most serious of them occurred in front of Bentley Hall, a mile and a-half out of Willenhall.

This was the last attempt at raising men on the old feudal levies; the trained bands were armed partly with pikes and partly with the newly-invented firelock, while the whole of the impressed men were armed merely with pikes. The Muster Roll for this immediate locality contains these names (that of Aspley is cancelled):—

	Traine.	Presse.
Tipton	Thomas Dudley,	—Thomas Winney. The L. dnd. —William Aspley pst. —John Winspurre in loco. —John Husband. —Joseph Richard. —William Dutton. —Richard Rushton: to be sp: per R. Turnor.
Darlaston & Bentley	Thomas Pye, Willm Turner,	
Wednesfield	John Hill,	
Willenhall	William Wilkes,	

Another Roll dated 1634, but apparently in use at this time, gives among the names of the "trayned horse" liable as (or for) 2 "curiasiers," "Thomas Levison, Esq.," and "Mrs. Lane and her sonne."

Within a couple of years Civil War had broken out in England, and Willenhall had to endure its full share of suffering lying, as it did, midway between two opposing strongholds—Dudley Castle, held for the King (under Colonel Leveson), and Rushall Hall, garrisoned for the Parliamentarian side.

Both sides in turn, as they were in a position to enforce payment, made levies of money upon the unfortunate inhabitants of the district. While Rushall Hall was a fortified position, first under its owner, Sir Edward Leigh, and afterwards under its military governor, Captain Tuthill, Willenhall was forced to pay to the support of the garrison there.

Here is the evidence of an official notice:—

> April 8th, 1643.—Ordered that the weekly pay, and five weeks' arrears, of Norton and Wirley, Pelsall, Rushall, and Goscote, Willenhall, Wednesfield and Wednesbury, shall be assigned to Col. Leigh for payment of his officers of horse and troopers

There is a similar military order, dated 22nd June, 1644, by which the weekly pay of all these places is assigned to Captain Tuthill, governor of Rushall, though in the parcelling out of contributory areas, Bushbury, Wolverhampton, Bilston, and Bradley are included in another district. The other side were employing forced labour for strengthening the defence of Dudley Castle, and not improbably the Leveson tenants from Wednesfield and Willenhall were impressed to go up there equipped with spade and mattock.

Doubtless troops and detachments of armed men were frequently to be seen passing through Willenhall; while Wolverhampton, owing to the influence of the Levesons and the Goughs, was almost a Royalist rallying place. Soon after the skirmish at Hopton Heath, near Stafford, in 1643, Charles I. found shelter in the old Star and Garter Inn (then in Cock Street), and to this hostelry came Mr. Henry Gough, who had accommodated Charles, Prince of Wales, and his younger brother, James, Duke of York, at his private residence, to proffer the King a willing war loan of £1,200.

The same year the King made the same hostelry his headquarters, dating a letter which he addressed to the Lichfield magistrates, directing them to send their arms to join the Royal standard at Nottingham, "Att our Court at Wolverhampton, 17 August, 1642."

In 1643, Prince Rupert, after his memorable fight at Birmingham, made an attack upon Rushall Hall; and notwithstanding the gallant defence of Mistress Leigh, in the absence of her husband, its lord, took and held it for the King, putting in as governor Sir Edward Leigh's neighbour, Colonel Lane, of Bentley. With a garrison of 100 to 200 men, he held Rushall Hall for some months, having some exciting times, chiefly in the plundering of the enemy's stores, and the private merchandise of carriers passing along the great Watling Street over Cannock Chase.

On May 10th, 1644, the Earl of Denbigh, after a vigorous attack, recaptured Rushall, finding there thousands of pounds' worth of stolen goods, and taking among other prisoners William Hopkins, of Oakeswell Hall, Wednesbury. It was then Captain Tuthill became commander of the garrison.

In the same month the Stafford Parliamentarian Committee ordered the seizure of all the horses and cattle belonging to that staunch Royalist, Squire Lane, and of all the other cavalier landowners around Bentley. The seizure was duly made, and realised by sale at Birmingham. As a set-off to this it must be recounted that at the beginning of the year Colonel Lane had fallen upon a Parliamentary escort convoying stores and provisions to Stafford, routed the enemy, and taken no less than sixty horses, fifty-five of their packs containing ammunition. Hence, the reprisal at this first opportunity.

In the September of the year (1644) a remarkable episode occurred. The governor of Dudley Castle, Sir Thomas Leveson, employed one of his trusty tenants, a yeoman named Francis Pitt, of Wednesfield, to make a secret attempt to bribe Captain Tuthill to betray Rushall and its garrison into his hands. A number of letters passed between Leveson and Tuthill, for the latter pretended from the outset to fall in with the treacherous proposal, with the object of recovering some prisoners; which having accomplished, he seized Pitt, the go-between, and delivered him up to the Parliament.

Colonel Leveson, unconscious of this treachery, came according to arrangement to Rushall, but instead of finding an easy entrance, had two "drakes," or small cannons, fired upon him, killing a number of his troops. The letters of Leveson and Tuthill will be found printed in full in Willmore's "History of Walsall." The unfortunate messenger, Francis Pitt, was tried in London by "Court Martial," and hanged at Smithfield on October 12th. It transpired at the trial that he was selected by Colonel Leveson because he held a farm of him for life, was familiar with Rushall Hall, and had told him he had to go there to pay his war contributions, and sometimes to redeem his neighbours' cattle. On the one side Captain Tuthill had promised him £100 of the £2,000 bribe by which it was proposed to seduce him, and on the other his landlord had offered to remit seven years of his rent. Such is the fortune of war, however, the poor wretch, instead of reward, met with an ignominious death at the age of 65, after a life of honest toil.

In 1645 Prince Rupert had his headquarters in Wolverhampton, while the King lay two miles to the north of the town, where tradition says he watched a skirmish with the enemy from Bushbury Hill. When Charles I. fled before Cromwell at Naseby on June 14th of that year he passed through Lichfield and entered Wolverhampton. After sleeping the night, either at the Old Hall, Robert Levenson's residence, or at a house in Old Lichfield Street, the unfortunately King passed on the next morning towards Bewdley.

Some interesting local information during this war time is to be derived from the literary remains of an officer in the King's Army, one Captain Symmonds, who amused himself on his marches by taking heraldic notes, and noticing monumental inscriptions. An entry in his Diary thus alludes to the foregoing facts:—

> Friday, May 16, 1645.
>
> The rendezvous was near the King's quarters. Began after 4 o'clock in the morning here. One soldier was hanged for mutiny.
>
> The prince's headquarters was at Wolverhampton. A handsome towne. One faire church in it.
>
> The King lay at Bisbury. A private sweet village where Squire Grosvenor (as they call him) lives. Which name hath continued here 120 years. Before him lived Bisbury of Bisbury.

Our military diarist next writes:—

> Satterday, May 17, 1645.—His Majestie marched from here to Tong—

and goes on to enumerate the garrisons in Staffordshire at that date, distinguishing by initials which were "Rebel" and which were the "King's"; among them:—

> K. Lichfield.—Colonel Bagott, governor.
>
> R. Russell hall.—A taylor governor.
>
> R. Mr. Gifford's house at Chillington, three miles from Wolverhampton. Now slighted by themselves.
>
> K. Dudley Castle.—Colonel Leveson, whose estate and habitation is at Wolverhampton, is governor.

"Slighted" signifies dismantled of its fortification; the allusion to "a tailor" being military governor of Rushall is, of course, a cavalier's sneer at the Republican soldiery.

Coming now to the end of the war, when Charles II. was defeated at Worcester in 1651, the country round Willenhall became the scene of that fugitive monarch's most romantic wanderings. Flying from the battlefield at the close of that fatal September day, Charles made his way through Stourbridge to Whiteladies and Boscobel. Then occurred the episode of his hiding in the "Royal Oak," and his concealment inside the house, in the "priests' hole" at the top of the stairs, by Mrs. Penderel.

Fearing discovery, the King was escorted by the brothers Penderel to Moseley Hall, near Bushbury, a timber-framed mansion in the picturesque Elizabethan style, the home of the Whitgreates, where the hunted monarch was welcomed and immediately refreshed with some biscuits and a bottle of sack. Charles had scarcely departed from Boscobel ere a troop of Roundheads arrived to search it. And another narrow escape now occurred at Moseley, where again a cunningly contrived hiding place was brought into requisition. Even after the frustration of the search party, one Southall, a notorious "priest catcher," called at the suspected house.

Prudence dictated another secret flight, and taking advantage of a dark night the unhappy King was taken by Colonel Lane to his own house, and was next hidden at Bentley Hall.

The story of the escape of Charles II. from Bentley towards the continent, disguised as a groom and riding in front of Jane Lane's pillion, is too well known to need re-telling here. The episode is historic; it is the subject of a fresco painted on the walls of a corridor in the gilded chambers of Parliament.

The whole romance of Boscobel and Bentley is told with considerable fulness in Shaw's "Staffordshire" (I., pp. 73–84), and is accompanied by very interesting engravings of Boscobel, Moseley Hall, and Old Bentley.

As a result of the Revolution of 1688, and with the death of Queen Anne in 1714, the impracticable Stuarts disappeared for good from the English throne; but as adherents to their discredited cause, known as Jacobites, still remained numerous, it may be guessed they were not lacking in and around Willenhall.

After the Hanoverian Succession there were, in fact, a number of avowed Jacobites in this vicinity, who refused to take the oath of allegiance to George I. Their names and behaviour were kept strictly under notice by the Government, but for fear of driving them to extremes no active measures were taken against them or their estates. A list of these non-jurors and

Roman Catholics was compiled after the rebellion of 1715, and again in 1745, when the rebellion of the Young Pretender once more disturbed the Kingdom. A list of these suspects was published on each occasion by the Government, with the amount of penalties incurred (but not exacted) against each name. In these lists appeared the following names:—

	£	s.	d.
Charles Smith, of Bushbury, Esq.	67	0	0
Anne Kempson, of Estington, widow	11	0	0
Ursula Kempson, of Wolverhampton, widow	39	0	0
John Kempson, of Great Sardon	41	0	0
William Ward, ditto	9	2	6
Mary Leveson, of Willenhall, in Wolverhampton	31	10	0
John Leveson, ditto	50	17	6
John Brandon, of Prestwood, yeoman	12	5	6
Thomas Giffard, of Chillington, Esq.	2100	6	6½
Elizabeth Giffard, of Wolverhampton, spinster	58	19	0
Thomas Whitgreaves, of Moseley, Esq.	73	2	6

XIV.—Litigation Concerning the Willenhall Prebend (1615–1702).

The Prebend had little to do with Willenhall, except in name. However, as the name of Willenhall was attached to this particular "canonical portion" in the Collegiate Church of Wolverhampton, and more especially as the Levesons are connected with its later history, reference to it cannot well be omitted.

The Leveson family had been dealing with Wolverhampton church property for centuries, and in the Stuart period were lessees of the greater part of it at a nominal rent of £38 per annum. Their standing in the county may be gauged by this entry which the Heralds made concerning the family at "Visitation" 1538:—

> Richard Leveson of Willenhall was living in 27 Edward I. He married Margereye, daughter of Henry Fitz Clemente of Wolverhampton.

By an indenture of the year 1613 the Dean and Chapter of Wolverhampton leased the deanery, prebends, and manor of Wolverhampton to Sir Walter Leveson, and all the lands belonging thereto in various parts of Staffordshire and Worcestershire, including those at Willenhall, Wednesfield, Bentley, &c., with all the mines of sea coal, ironstone, &c., on the said premises, but specially excepting the patronage and gifts of prebends, canonship, and all their offices and ecclesiastical jurisdiction; all at an annual reserved rent of £38, and the quaint old-world tenure of having "to entertain the Dean and his retinue two days and three nights in each year."

The validity of these leases was questioned a few years later in the 13th year of James I., the lessee having refused to pay the reserved rents without considerable deductions; and a bill was filed in Chancery by Joseph Hall, D.D., prebendary of Willenhall, and Christopher Cragg, prebendary of Hatherton (probably on the advice of the newly installed Dean, Dr. Anthony Maxey), against the aforesaid, Sir Walter Leveson, who was then in possession of the property belonging to their two prebends, as well as other possessions belonging to the College of Wolverhampton.

Although the case was decided against Sir Walter Leveson, the prebendaries reaped little or no benefit; for Sir Walter died immediately after, leaving his heir a minor, and a ward of the King. During the wardship the King attempted to settle the questions and controversies which had arisen when he made the appointment of a new Dean.

It must be borne in mind that the Deans of Wolverhampton were also Deans of Windsor; and Dr. Maxey dying about 1618, there followed a somewhat quick succession of Deans. These were Matthew Wren (1628), protege of Laud, and successively Bishop of Hereford, of Norwich, and of Ely; Christopher Wren, his brother (1634), father of the famous architect of the same name; Dr. Bruno Ryes (1660); and Dr. Brideoak, who became Bishop of Chichester in 1675.

The wardship of young Leveson lasted 16 years, and when he came of age the prebendaries were glad to come to a composition with him.

By this composition he agreed to pay them £30 per annum each, in full satisfaction of the several tithes and other profits belonging in right to their respective prebends; this being over and above the said reserved rents which had been previously paid. Arrangements were made at the same time with the rest of the prebendaries respecting the several proportions of the tithe belonging to them.

About this time the Dean and Prebendaries successfully resisted an attempt of the Archbishop of Canterbury to hold a visitation within the "peculiar"— the church's jurisdiction within itself.

After the Civil War the Prebendaries found that they had suffered considerable losses by the acts of their predecessors; so it was determined by Thomas Wren, LL.D. (son of the aforementioned Rev. Matthew Wren, Bishop of Ely, whose literary remains include "A Brief History of the Parish and Jurisdiction of Wolverhampton, from the Time of King Edgar") prebendary of Willenhall, and Cæsar Callendine, B.D., prebendary of Hatherton, to file a bill in Chancery against Robert Leveson for a discovery of the lands he held which anciently belonged to the prebendaries of Wolverhampton, and that he might show by what title he held them.

The hearing was before the great Lord Chancellor of that day, Lord Clarendon, who dismissed the bill, though without costs.

The Leveson family consequently continued in the undisturbed enjoyment of the church property, granted to them in fee farm by six prebendaries, as well as of divers other freehold estates in the parish of Wolverhampton.

The Leveson property in Wolverhampton became much implicated in the numerous family settlements till, in 1702, Frances, Earl of Bradford, purchased it of Robert Leveson for £22,000. Lord Bradford also acquired, three years later, the estate of the Dean and Prebends of Wolverhampton which had been leased to the Earl of Windsor; so that the entire property of the Collegiate Church (except the prebendal houses and some property which had been set aside for the use of the Sacrist), passed into the hands of one and the same proprietor.

In the same year, however, the Dean, Prebendaries, and Sacrist filed a bill in Chancery against Leveson and the Earl for the recovery of the property. The plaintiffs were Gregory Hascard, D.D., dean; Prebendaries John Hinton (Willenhall), Richard Redding (Kinvaston), Thomas Allestree (Hilton), John Plimley (Fetherstone), John Hilman (Hatherton), Richard Ames (Monmore), Walter Ashley (Wobaston), and Henry Wood, sacrist.

They contended they were all clerks, constituted one entire body, and rector or parson incorporate, of the whole parish of Wolverhampton, which was of very great extent, consisting of 16 or 17 hamlets or villages besides the large town of Wolverhampton, being in circuit about thirty miles, in three of which said hamlets there were chapels of ease, the several cures thereof belonging to the said College or Free Chapel Royal.

In all this litigation it was a question much agitated whether, as all the prebendaries with the Dean and the Sacrist constituted one entire body, any single prebendary could demise his annual portion of the said general tithes without the consent of the whole body.

The defendant Leveson was accused of having contrived secret conveyances of many parcels of the said tithes and lands for the benefit of his own family, some of the properties having been sold for large sums of money, and the church revenues defrauded thereby. Also that he had so altered and confounded the buildings, fences, and boundaries of the church lands, and so mixed them up with his own inherited lands, that it had become impossible to discern or distinguish which were the original possessions of the College; possessions which at the Domesday Survey had extended to 3,000 acres, besides the lordship of Lutley, near Halesowen.

Dr. Oliver states that in his time (1836) there remained some "houses and lands now belonging to the prebendaries and Sacrist, which are leased out for lives."

The "corpses" of the six prebends are supposed to have consisted of the tithes of their respective districts in Willenhall, Hilton, Hatherton, Fetherston, Monmore, and Wobaston.

The Rev. Richard Ames, Curate of Bilston for 46 years (1684–1730), makes the following record:—

> 1723, December 9th.—The Reverd. Mr. Wm. Craddock, Rector of Donnington (Salop), was installed Prebendary of Willenhall, he having resigned that of Hatherston. The mandate for his installmt. was directed to me (ye Senior Prebendary) by ye Rt. Hon'ble George, Lord Willoughby de Broke, Deane of o'r Collegiate Church of Wolverhampton, and of Windsor; I being constituted locum tenens.

On ye 10th December, 1723, by virtue of an'r mandate to me, directed by ye same Ld. Willoughby de Broke, ye same Mr. Wm. Craddock was by me put in possession of ye Sacrist's Stall, both which places became vacant by ye death of Mr. Hinton. He (Mr. Craddock) was also constituted principal official.

In 1836, when Dr. Oliver wrote his history of the church, the Chapter of the College consisted of the Hon. Henry Lewis Hobart, D.D. (Dean), the Rev. R. Ellison, M.A., prebendary of Willenhall, and the other prebendaries (of Kinvaston, Hilton, Featherston, Monmore, Hatherton, and Wobaston respectively), and the Rev. G. Oliver, D.D., perpetual curate and Sacrist (an Act obtained in 1811 by Dean Legge had constituted the Sacrist the real incumbent of the church). The Chapter had it own seal, which was of proper ecclesiastical design, and of some antiquity.

On the death of the very Rev. and Hon. H. L. Hobart, D.C.L., &c., in 1846, the Collegiate establishment of Wolverhampton ceased to exist, and its property became vested in the ecclesiastical Commissioners.

Such was the gross abuse of ecclesiastical patronage, the entire income of the Collegiate Church (except £100 a year for a curate of very indefinite status) had been absorbed in the payment of a Dean of the two "peculiars" of Windsor and Wolverhampton, and of some half-dozen legendary prebendaries who were for the most part unknown, even by name, to the oldest inhabitant of the parish.

With the suppression of the ancient Deanery, the modern township of Wolverhampton was divided into thirteen ecclesiastical parishes.

XV.—Willenhall Struggling to be a Free Parish.

In the eighteenth century the ecclesiastical history of Willenhall reached a critical stage. Long and bitter were the disputes which arose between the mother church of Wolverhampton and the daughter chapelries of Willenhall and Bilston; and perhaps the temper of the authorities at the former had not been improved by the gradual impoverishment of the residentiaries there, the history of which formed the subject of the last chapter.

The first cause of the quarrel was found in the fact that these two places, having become as populous as towns of ordinary status, were without legal burying-grounds. When land had been provided there seems to have been considerable hesitancy on the part of the authorities in allowing Willenhall and Bilston these ordinary parochial privileges. The Rev. Richard Ames, of Bilston, has left it on record that on June 9th, 1726, he waited upon the Bishop of the diocese, while he was holding a confirmation at Walsall, when "John Lane, Esqre., of Bentley, mov'd his lordship to consecrate Willenhall and Bilston Chapelyards for burial-places, wch. his lordship seemed inclinable to do."

The history of the conflict goes back to 1709, when Dr. Manningham, on becoming Dean, convened a Chapter at Oxford which was attended by all the Prebendaries and the Sacrist. This meeting was specially called to consider the case of the inhabitants of Willenhall and Bilston, who had represented to the Dean the great inconveniences which arose in having to carry their dead from these chapelries for interment at Wolverhampton; and humbly praying that their respective chapels and chapelyards should be consecrated for the proper burial of the dead.

The prayer was granted, but it was most carefully stipulated that the inhabitants of the two chapelries should always pay the customary levies to the mother church, and also the fees for burials and for the churching of women, to the respective curates of the said chapels, as well as to the ministers of the mother church; and that the expenses attending the desired consecrations should be paid by the petitioners.

A subsequent Chapter, held 10 October, 1718, confirmed this, when the Ministers and Inhabitants of the Chapelries of Bilston and Willenhall signed an Agreement to observe and perform the said conditions. For the carrying out of the agreement in business-like form the said Ministers covenanted to pay the said fees half-yearly, at Lady-day and Michaelmas, transmitting a copy of their respective Registers "without reserve or fraud" to be transcribed into the books of the mother church.

The fees to be charged each Chapelry were fixed to a scale: tenpence for "ye churching of every woman"; sevenpence for the burial of each body in the churchyard, and twice that amount for the burial inside the church: and so on.

Subsequently (some 30 years after, when St. John's Chapel, Wolverhampton, was in contemplation) the inhabitants of the Liberties of Willenhall and Bilston, notwithstanding the written agreement aforesaid, peremptorily and finally refused to pay their respective fees for Christenings, Churchings, and Burials to the Sacrist and Curates of Wolverhampton; payments whereby the profits of their several offices were lessened more than half, and the loss was so considerable it was no longer to be borne.

At Bilston the quarrel of 1753 was practically not settled for nearly a century afterwards. It was ruled that whatever might be arranged in respect of fees for other rites no marriages could be legally performed in the Chapel except by licence of Wolverhampton, which claimed a "Peculiar" jurisdiction; and as the inhabitants indignantly refused to pay double marriage fees, no marriage was solemnised in the chapel from January, 1754, to February, 1841.

The same year—to be exact, the date was April 12th, 1841—the first marriage was solemnised at Willenhall Church, the Bishop having then issued a special licence to the Incumbent to marry persons living within the township.

Almost concurrently with this dispute there was another source of grievance to Willenhall, Bilston, and Pelsall which had to be strenuously fought by these outlying places.

This quarrel arose, in the main, through the excessive demands made upon the inhabitants of the three chapelries for rates with which to repair and maintain the fabric of Wolverhampton Church. The levies made ostensibly for this purpose seem to have been at times somewhat exorbitant, and the money to have been spent in meeting charges which can only be described as superfluous so far as the non-residential contributors were concerned.

About 1738 the chapelwardens of Bilston made a determined stand against the churchwardens of Wolverhampton.

A "case was stated" in which it was shown that the Collegiate Church of Wolverhampton consisted of a Dean and Prebendaries, founded by a Royal Family, and was subject to no visitation but that of the Crown. It contained three Chapels—one at Bilston, another at Willenhall, and a third at Pelsall.

The statement proceeded:—"Every Hamlet and Village in the Ecclesiastical Parish of Wolverhampton has a Constable and all other parochial officers, and maintains its own poor as it were a separate parish. . . ."

"The Chapelries of Willenhall and Bilston nominate and maintain each its own Clergy, and repair their own Chapels, which have been endowed time out of mind, and were consecrated about thirteen years ago for burying places."

Other points of complaint put forward were that the two chapels afforded every facility to the inhabitants of the respective places for divine worship and the administration of the sacraments; that formerly Bilston and Willenhall each paid only £4 a year to the mother church, but that since 1716 increasing demands had been made till as much as £56 was asked for; and that all which these chapelries received in return were the bread and wine used in the sacrament, four times a year, and for which they paid £4 per annum, the chapelwardens being allowed 3d. in the £ at Boston and 4d. in the £ at Willenhall for collecting it.

It was also complained that all the rest of the villages had been forced "to contribute in like proportion with these two towns," and that these levies on the out-hamlets had been made for additions to, or improvements of, Wolverhampton Church, which were quite superfluous in their character, if not absolutely illegal.

On this opinion (of a learned Sergeant-at-Law) the inhabitants of Willenhall were invited to join with those of Bilston in a common defence for their mutual benefit. On the advice of the esteemed Dr. Wilkes, a well-known local Antiquary, who was then the leading public man of Willenhall, the invitation was declined.

Litigation proceeded for several years both in the ecclesiastical courts and in chancery, but without any definite decision being arrived at.

In 1754 the Earl of Stamford tried to induce both parties to submit a case fairly drawn up (for the legal work in the preparation of which he generously offered to pay all the costs) and to abide by the decision. The people of Willenhall, through Dr. Wilkes, thanked his lordship for his friendly offer, and declared their willingness to accept it.

The Wolverhampton officials, however, rejected the proposal, in the hope they would win their case in the ecclesiastical courts. When the case eventually came to trial in 1755 an old parish book was produced, which showed that the exorbitant demands of Wolverhampton were distinctly illegal. In it was an entry of 1668, which ran in this wise:—

"This is the portion of Rates each Chapelry and Prebend shall pay towards the repairs of the Mother Church:—

	£	s.	d.
Wolverhampton	36	0	0
Bilston	12	0	0
Wylnale	12	0	0
Wednesflde	12	0	0
Hatherton	3	0	0
Featherstone	1	4	0
Kinvaston	1	1	0
Hilton	1	7	0
Pelsall	2	2	0
Bentley	1	10	0
Stretton rent	1	6	8
	83	10	8

A writ of prohibition was forthwith filed to stay all further proceedings in the Spiritual Courts; and the law costs of the trial, amounting to £282 1s. 8d., were divided equally between Bilston and Willenhall (1756).

XVI.—Dr. Richard Wilkes, of Willenhall (1690–1760).

Willenhall's most illustrous son was Dr. Richard Wilkes, Antiquary, whose house still stands on the Walsall Road. He came of good family of county rank, and his personal character raised him to the eminence of a notability in Staffordshire. His portrait appears in Shaw's history of this county of which his (Wilkes') valuable and voluminous MSS. formed the nucleus. Though settled in this locality, adding to their little patrimony from time to time for 300 or 400 years, the family came originally from Hertfordshire.

The pedigree of Wilkes, according to the Heralds' Visitation in 1614, commences with John Wylkys de Darlaston, who was witness to a Deed of Roger, Lord of Darlaston, in the time of Edward III. (1331). There is a Richard Wylkys, of Willenhall, who witnessed a Bentley Deed in 1413. To this Richard and his wife Juliana, daughter and heir of William Wilkes, a grant of lands in Bentley was made by Humphrey, Earl of Stafford. The son of this couple was William Wilkes of Willnall (1505). Protonotary of the Court of Common Pleas, 15 Henry VIII. The family tree is very complete in Shaw.

One John Wilkes married a widow Parkhouse, *nee* Margery Garbet, of Nether Penn; another John, his nephew, was Rector of Lum, and evidently a Puritan, as his two sons bear the striking biblical names, Ephraim and Manasses. Richard seems to have been the favourite name for the eldest son. One Richard married Mercy Drakeford, of Stafford (see Salt. Vol. VIII.); his son, also named Richard, became the father of our Willenhall worthy, whose mother was Lucretia, youngest daughter of Jonas Astley, of Wood Eaton, in this county.

Richard Wilkes, M.D., was born in March, 1690, and had his school education at Trentham. In his 19th year he was entered at St. John's College, Cambridge, and was admitted scholar 1710. In April, 1711, he began to attend Mr. Saunderson's mathematical lectures, and became very proficient in algebra. In January, 1713, he took his B.A degree; three years later he was chosen Fellow, and in 1718 he was appointed Linacre Lecturer.

It does not appear when or where he took his degrees in medicine. He seems to have taken pupils and taught mathematics in college from the year 1715 till he left it, and to have been engaged thus early in literary matters, particularly in the collection of material for subsequent use. It was by his literary labours, particularly in antiquarian research, that he made himself a name.

He presently took deacon's orders, and once preached in the parish church of Wolverhampton. He also preached several times at Stow, near Chartley. However, disappointment in the expectation of preferment in the

Church soon disgusted him with the ministry, and in 1720 he began to practise physic, for which he seemed to have a natural talent, at Wolverhampton. In 1725 he married Rachel Manlove, of Abbots Bromley, with whom he had a handsome fortune, and from that time he dwelt with his father (who died in 1730) at Willenhall.

About this time he wrote an excellent treatise on Dropsy; and later, when a dreadful disease raged among the horned cattle of the Midlands, he published a very useful and practical "Letter to Breeders and Graziers in the County of Stafford," and made every effort to assist in stamping out the plague. Possibly while at Chartley he had made a study of the herd of wild cattle preserved there.

His skill as a physician was very considerable, and seems to have been applied chiefly to the gratuitous relief of his poorer neighbours. He led an exemplary life, being an early riser, and an indefatigable reader, constantly adding to the rich stores of his well-stocked mind.

As previously mentioned, he spent several years of industry in collecting historical manuscripts, and making antiquarian notes relating to his native county, of which the Rev. Stebbing Shaw afterwards made such good use.

For instance, Dr. Wilkes' account of Roman roads, camps, and other remains of antiquity is a fairly exhaustive one for a county history, and shows a considerable depth of research. It is embodied in the "Introduction" and the "General History" at the commencement of Shaw's compendious work.

Like Pepys, he kept a Diary, which was never intended for publication—he was a diligent recorder of historical facts. Here is an interesting note from it:—

> "The first steam engine that ever raised any quantity of water was erected near Wolverhampton, on the right-hand side of the road leading to Walsall, over against the half-mile stone." (This was on the site of the Chillington ironworks.)

The Diarist was too modest to add that the Waterworks which long supplied Wolverhampton with water were the property of Dr. Wilkes.

Among other projected literary works was a new edition of Hudibras, with notes, &c. In the beginning of the year 1747, having a severe fit of illness which confined him to the house, he amused himself with writing his own epitaph, which he calls "A picture drawn from the life without heightening." It is as follows:—

> Here, reader, stand awhile, and know
> Whose carcase 'tis that rots below;
> A man's, who walk'd by Reason's rule

> Yet sometimes err'd and play'd the fool;
> A man's sincere in all his ways,
> And full of the Creator's praise,
> Who laughed at priestcraft, pride and strife,
> And all the little tricks of life.
> He lov'd his king, his country more,
> And dreadful party-rage forbore:
> He told nobility the truth
> And winked at hasty slips of youth.
> The honest poor man's steady friend.
> The villain's sconce in hopes to mend.
> His father, mother, children, wife,
> His riches, honour, length of life,
> Concern not thee. Observe what's here—
> He rests in hope and not in fear.

His wife dying in May, 1756, he married for the second time in October the same year Mrs. Frances Bendish (sister to the Rev. Sir Richard Wrottesley, of Wrottesley, Bart.), who long survived him, dying December 24, 1798, at Froxfield, near Petersfield, in Hampshire, at a very advanced age.

The learned doctor himself died March 6, 1760, with a return of the gout in his stomach, and his death was universally lamented by his tenants, who lost an indulgent landlord; by his servants, who lost a good master; but more by numbers of poor in the populous villages adjacent and at a distance, in grateful remembrance of the charitable advice and friendly assistance they had always enjoyed at his kindly hands. A somewhat eulogistic entry of his death appears in the Bilston Registers.

As Dr. Wilkes left no issue, his property passed to the Unett family, the representatives of his aunt Anne who had married George Unett, of Wolverhampton.

He was buried at Willenhall in his native soil, where a neat monument was erected to his memory near the family pew, by his heirs, Captain Richard Wilkes Unett, and Mr. John Wilkes Unett; the tablet was thus inscribed:—

> "Near this place
> Lie the remains
> of
> RICHARD WILKES, M.D.
>
> Formerly fellow of St. John's College, Cambridge; the last of an ancient and respectable family resident at this place 300 years and upwards. He married first, Rachel, eldest

daughter of Rowland Manlove, of Lees Hill, in this county, esq.; secondly, Frances, daughter of Sir John, and sister

of the late
Sir Richard Wrottesly, of Wrottesly, Bart.
and widow of Higham Bendish, Esq.
He died March 6, 1760,
aged 70 years.

[Underneath is the following escutcheon:—

(Wilkes) Paly of eight Or and Gules; on a chief Argent, three lozenges of the second: impaling, 1. (Manlove) Azure, a chevron Ermine, between three anchors Argent; 2. (Wrottesley) Or, three piles Sa. a canton Ermine]

"The children of the late Rev. Thomas Unett, of Stafford, his heirs-at-law, placed this monument an. 1800."

On the floor of the Lane Chapel in Wolverhampton Church will be found stones to the memory of the Wilkes family, "seated at Willenhall from the reign of Edward IV."; there is also a blue slab to the memory of Mary Unett, who died in 1767.

The old house of Dr. Wilkes, a good specimen of its type of architecture, stands back from the main road behind iron palisading. Part of it has been utilised as a stamper's warehouse; had it received the respect due to its associations, it might flittingly have been a town Museum, or some such public institution. It was built by the Doctor's father, and the Doctor was born there.

The house has a white stuccoed front, irregularly disposed, the semi-porticoed doorway with classic columns having three windows on its left and two on its right, although the shorter side seems to have been lengthened at a later period by a red brick wing. Along the line of the first floor are six windows, whose lights in the Annean period, to which the building belongs, were doubtless of small leaded panes.

From the tiled roof project three dormers, the centre one having a semi-circular head, the outer ones pointed. The chimneys stand out from each gable end, and in the brickwork of each of their sides is a plain recessed panel; the chimney-heads being noticeable for the absence of the usual projecting courses. Local tradition says that Hall street was once a stately avenue of trees by which this residence was approached from Lichfield Street.

On entering the house, the visitor feels a pang of regret that the venerable building should ever have been degraded to the purposes of commerce; particularly as the fabric retains many of its characteristics, thanks to the soundness of the workmanship of two centuries ago. The decorations in the form of plaster mouldings that cover the beams, and the medallion or panel pictures, being partly historical and partly classical, all exhibit the Renaissance feeling of the early eighteenth century.

The ceilings of two lower rooms are in a splendid state of preservation, and contain excellent work. One room is square with beams across the middle; the ceiling on one side of the beam representing "The Seasons," and on the other side "The Elements." The Seasons are severally depicted as follows:— A young face, with the hair of the head bedecked with flowers, for "Spring"; a face in the bloom of womanhood, with the hair bedecked with corn, represents "Summer"; a well-matured face, having the hair bedecked with fruit, "Autumn"'; while a pleasing aged face, the brow bedecked with holly, stands for "Winter." Painted on the wall over the fireplace is the Castle of St. Angelo, and the bridge crossing the Tiber at Rome. The Elements, (so called by the old alchemists) are also figuratively, represented by four heads; one bearing a castle, with three towers and other buildings in the background (Earth); one surmounted by an eagle with outspread wings (Air); the next with tongues of fire issuant (Fire); and the other spouting forth a fountain (Water).

The other room is oblong, with beams across dividing its ceiling into four parts. In these parts there are four well-drawn figures, one believed to be Bacon, with beard, moustache, whiskers, and in Elizabethan costume; two close cropped heads, carried on noble necks, believed to be respectively Julius Cæsar and Mark Antony; and the fourth is said to be Homer, with the customary curly hair and beard, but showing a collar of some sort, and apparently wearing a skull cap. Over the mantel, painted on canvas, is the Coliseum, showing the Arch of Titus and a pool in the foreground.

In the main room upstairs is still to be seen the portrait of Dr. Wilkes, painted on canvas, over the mantelpiece. He is depicted as a clean shaven man with benevolent face, bluish or blue-grey eyes, a good forehead, nose, mouth and chin well-defined, and wearing a wig. His costume includes a high-cut waistcoat, bearing ten buttons, opened in front nearly all the way down to show cravat and frilled shirt, the cravat having a buckle—probably jewelled in front. The outer coat is without a collar, cut a little lower than the waistcoat, sloping from above outwards, showing eight buttons, and apparently of greenish-brown velvet.

The pool which formerly ornamented the garden had disappeared; but the boathouse is still there, and the room above it in which the Doctor used to keep his Antiquarian Collection and other artistic treasures. As to the lawns, shrubberies, gardens, orchards, and pleasaunces, there is scarcely a remnant left.

Of the once sweet and pellucid stream, spanned by an ornamental bridge, which conducted the rambler to the pleasant meads beyond, nothing remains but the name, "Willenhall Brook"—it is now little better than a dirty open sewer.

It may not be generally known that a passing allusion is made to Wilkes in Boswell's "Life of Johnson."

In the IV. chapter of Vol. I. of this monumental biography we read that in 1740 Dr. Johnson wrote "an epitaph on Phillips, a musician, which was afterwards published with some other pieces of his, in 'Mrs. Williams's Miscellanies.' This epitaph is so exquisitely beautiful, that I remember even Lord Kaines, strangely prejudiced as he was against Dr. Johnson, was compelled to allow it very high praise. It has been ascribed to Mr. Garrick from its appearing at first with the signature G; but I have heard Mr. Garrick declare it was written by Dr. Johnson, and give the following account of the manner in which it was composed. Johnson and he were sitting together, when amongst other things Garrick repeated an epitaph upon this Phillips, by a Dr. Wilkes, in these words:—

> Exalted soul! whose harmony could please
> The love-sick virgin, and the gouty ease;
> Could jarring discord, like Amphion, move
> To beauteous order and harmonious love;
> Rest here in peace, till angels bid thee rise
> And meet thy blessed Saviour in the skies.

"Johnson shook his head at the common-place funeral lines, and said to Garrick, 'I think, Davy, I can make better.'"

The great biographer goes on to state that Johnson, after stirring about his tea and meditating a little while, produced these lines:—

> Exalted soul! thy various sounds could please
> The love-sick virgin, and the gouty ease;
> Could jarring crowds, like old Amphion, move
> To beauteous order and harmonious love.
> Rest here in peace, till angels bid thee rise,
> And join thy Saviour's concert in the skies.

Suffice it to add that the personage who inspired the lines was an eccentric genius named Claudius Phillips [88], on whose memorial tablet in the porch of Wolverhampton Church were engraved the said lines, attributed to Dr. Wilkes, who strangely enough is described as "of Trinity College, Oxford and Rector of Pitchford, Salop"—a clergyman whose name was John, and who lived a century previously. We are further informed that our Willenhall worthy is spoken of by Browne Willis in the "History of Mitred Abbies,"

Vol. II. p. 189—Browne Willis being one of the most notable antiquarians of that period, and an eccentric individual withal.

All this points to the fact that Dr. Richard Wilkes was well known as a writer, and acknowledged as an authority.

XVII.—Willenhall "Spaw."

It is difficult to imagine Willenhall as a health resort; yet it was no fault of Dr. Richard Wilkes that his native spot did not become a fashionable inland watering place.

It should be explained that during the eighteenth century there was almost a mania to discover and exploit wells and springs, and to regard them as fountains of health to which the fashionable and the well-to-do might be attracted. Before the newer fashion of sea bathing was introduced—which was early in the next century—there was a great number of these newly-invented places of inland resort. For instance, Dudley had its charming Spa on Pensnett Chace; and to show that Wolverhampton was not behindhand, we take the liberty of quoting from the MSS. of Dr. Wilkes:

> "A medical spring has lately been discovered at Chapel Ash, in the south-west part of this town, which purges moderately and without the least uneasiness. A brown ocre, or absorbent earth, remains after evaporation, mixt with salt and sulphur; so that it seems to promise relief in all kinds of disorders proceeding from costiveness, and alcaline, fiery, and acid humours in the stomach and bowels, attended by a flow of feverish heat, eruptions on the skin called scorbutic, headaches, giddiness, flatulency, sour eructations, flying pains called nervous and rheumatic, the hemorrhoids or piles, asthma, and many other disorders which seem incurable by the most powerful medicines."

Truly the Doctor might have earned a good living nowadays by writing the advertisements for modern quack specifics.

Shaw's description of the Willenhall Spa says that "the spring arises on the north side of a brook which runs almost directly from the west to the east, and so very near to it that a moderate shower will raise the brook as to cover it. About 200 yards up this brook, on the same side, are several springs, one of which was much taken notice of by our ancestors, and consecrated to St. Sunday, no common saint. Over it is the following inscription:—

> Fons occulis morbisque
> cutaneis diu celebris, A.D. 1726."

"Saint Sunday" must have been some local saint; or, more probably, a jocular embodiment of the sacredness of this day of the week with its peculiarly pagan name, to the cause of idleness, and so dubbed by the native wit of Willenhall; anyway, no saint of this name is to be found in the authorised Calendar of any church.

One of the Wilkes MSS. utilised by Shaw, and dated 1737, records the following experiment worked by the learned doctor with the local mineral waters:—

> "I evaporated in a brass furnace 13½ gallons to 3 quarts, then let it stand 3 days to settle, and poured the clear water from the fœces. This was a light smooth insipid earth of a yellow colour, fat between the fingers, insipid and impalpable, which being dried, weighed 93 grains. The remaining 3 quarts I evaporated in a brass kettle and had from it 53 grains of a very salt glutinous substance which dried into a solid mass of a brown colour. When the water came to a pint or thereabout, it began to smell like glew, and continued to do so when in a solid substance; it was then also as high-coloured as lye; but I am afraid this colour might arise from the brass kettle, in some measure, or too great a fire, being perhaps burnt."

Another of his scientific records runs:—

> "Oct. 9th.—I put into a Florence flask as much of this water as filled it up to the neck within 5 inches of the top. This I placed in a sand heat and increased the fire gradually till it boiled; and so I evaporated ad siccitatem. Some volatile sal stuck to the glass even up to the top; at the bottom was a small quantity of dark coloured matter, like that above, but I could not get together 2 grains of either. Here it is plain this sal is so volatile as to be raised and fly away by heat."

In another place he writes:—

> "On the 5th of November, 1737, I filled several glasses with this water, and put into them the following simples:—
>
> 1. Green Tea. This, in about 24 hours, made it of the colour of sack, and, by standing, it became much deeper coloured, like strong old beer.
>
> 2. Fustic; not so deep, more like cyder.
>
> 3. Red Sanders; almost the same colour in the light; but if I held the glass in the shade, it appeared of a blueish green, exactly like some old glass bottles I have formerly seen.
>
> 4. Alkanet; deeper, like old mountain wine.
>
> 5. Galls; paler than any of the foregoing. A large blue scum on the top, such as we see upon urine in fevers, and standing

lakes of water, where there are minerals. With logwood, tormentil, cort, granat, etc., there are some spots of this kind, but with none so much as with galls.

"A little below the Spaw (continues our authority), on the other side of the brook, they meet with a white clay, full of yellow veins of a deep colour, like gumboge when it has been for some time exposed to the air. These two they temper together and make into cakes, which they sell to the glovers by the name of ochre cakes, and with them they give a yellow colour to leather.

"Near the surface of the earth the country is for the most part a strong clay, which makes good brick, but, for a small compass from this Spaw all along the village on the north side of the brook we have sand. Underground the whole country abounds with coal and ironstone."

The glovers' handicraft, it may be mentioned in passing, was once strongly represented in olden Darlaston.

The situation of Willenhall is by no means an elevated one, and the whole plain in which it is situated formerly abounded in Springs, ere the surface had been so much disturbed by mining operations.

On the edge of the valley, under the shadow of Sedgley Beacon, was the famous Spring known as the Lady Wulfruna's, and which gave the place its name, Spring Vale; from this spot the silvery stream flowed eastwards into Willenhall, seeking the cool shade of the pleasant woodland there.

The stream, as it came in from Bilston, and ran eastwards through Willenhall, till it met the Tame, was once called the Hind Brook, or Stag River. In Saxon times the Tame here seems to have been designated Beorgita's Stream; and Mr. G. T. Lawley, in his "History of Bilston," says that the original bed of this brook was discovered in Willenhall some years ago when extensive excavations were being made.

So far the scientific aspect of this once famous Well. The popular view of a much frequented mineral spring which had "long been celebrated for disease of the eye and skin" opens out an even wider aspect. As previously mentioned, the brook flowing past it ran from west to east; a stream so directed was always accounted by the Druids of old as a sacred watercourse. Being thus from the earliest dawn of history within sacred precincts, there can be little doubt the Willenhall fountain enjoyed the reputation of a "Holy well" for many centuries. As such it came in for the annual custom of "well dressing," a vestige of the old pagan practice of well worship. Respecting this ancient custom, Dr. Plot, writing in 1686 in his "Natural History of Staffordshire," says:—

> "They have a custom in this county, which I observed on Holy Thursday at Brewood and Bilbrook, of adorning their Wells with boughs and flowers; this it seems they do at all gospel places, whether wells, trees, or hills, which being now observed only for decency and custom's sake, is innocent enough. Heretofore, too, it was usual to pay their respect to such wells as were eminent for curing distempers (one of which was at Wolverhampton in a narrow lane leading to a house, called Sea-well; another at Willenhall; others at Monmore Green, near Wolverhampton; at Codsall and many other parts of Staffordshire) on the saint's day whose name the well bore; diverting themselves with cakes and ale, and a little music and dancing; which, whilst within bound, was also an innocent recreation."

Dr. Oliver says the beautiful spring at Dunstall was the favourite resort of the Lady Wulfruna, and from contact with her sanctity acquired a reputation for possessing healing virtues of a miraculous character, and that this fountain was long known among its devotees as Wulfruna's Well.

Pitt's "History of Staffordshire," issued in 1817, gives a long list of local wells bearing at that time some similar repute for their remedial waters. Among them was Codsall Well, near Codsall Wood, supposed in olden times to be efficacious in cases of leprosy, and adjacent to which once stood a Leper House, replaced at a later period by a "Brimstone Ale-house," so-called because the water was sulphureous. The waters of the Monmore Green Well are described as containing "sulphur combined with vitriol." The Sea-well Spring still retained its name as a "Spaw" famous for its "eye water"; while those of Willenhall and Bentley were said to yield a valuable remedial sulphur water so long as they "could be kept from mixture with other waters."

Folklore not only connected these Wells with patron saints, but associated their magic precincts and curative effects with beneficent fairies. A well like that of Willenhall, which in a post-renaissance period was honoured with a stone frontal bearing a Latin inscription, would of a certainty be attended by fairy elves in an earlier and more primitive era.

> About this Spring (if ancient fame say true)
> The dapper elves their midnight sports pursue;
> Their pigmy king and little fairy queen,
> In circling dances gambolled on the green,

While tuneful sprites a merry concert made
And airy music warbled through the shade.

XVIII.—The Benefice.

Owing to the meagreness of the record, a complete list of the holders of the benefice is not to be expected. Thomas de Trollesbury has been named as "the parson of Willenhall" in 1297 (Chapter VII.); while we also have the names of three chantry priests here—William in the Lone, 1341 (Chapter XI.); Thomas Browning, "chaplain of the chantry" in 1397 (Chapter VII.); and Hugh Bromehall in 1526 (Chapter X.); all of them doubtless nominees of the Deanery of Wolverhampton.

Of course, it was possible, though not often the practice, for the holder of the living to act as "chaunter" priest as well. The Chantry endowments, as we have seen, were forfeited at the Reformation, at which period the benefice was returned as of the annual value of "£10 clear."

Either of these notorious evil-livers mentioned in Chapter XI., the non-preaching "dumb-dogs," Mounsell and Cooper, may have been the occupant of the Willenhall curacy in 1586. In 1609 an improvement in the intellectual status of the holder had been effected, William Padmore, D.D., being then incumbent.

In a previous chapter it was shown that the Rev. T. Badland was expelled from the living of Willenhall in 1662. It can now be shown that he was holding the benefice at least as early as 1658—and possibly from the beginning of the Cromwellian rule and the overthrow of the Episcopacy in 1646.

About 1645–6 ordinances were passed appointing a Committee to consider ways and means of upholding and settling the maintenance of ministers in England and Wales. In 1654 the powers of the Plundered Ministers' Committee were transferred to the Trustees for Maintenance. The Committee took the receipts of all Tithes, Fifths, and First Fruits; and later on the income of the rectories, bishoprics, deaneries, and chapters; they sold the bishops' lands, &c.

It was out of this income that augmentations and advances were granted by the said Committee to ministers and school-masters. In the Record Office at London there is an audited account the Treasurer to the "Trustees for the Maintenance of Ministers and other pious uses of moneys," showing among the disbursements for the year ending 26 December, 1658, one to

"Thomas Badland, of Willenhall (6 months to 1659, March 25) ... £10."

In curious contrast with this high-minded clergyman, who sacrificed his living to his conscience, is his successor in the Curacy of Willenhall, the Rev. Mr. Gilpin, who had to be seriously admonished for non-residence and other faults, and was at last, in the year 1674, turned out of the living altogether. Not improbably this gentleman was a pluralist, an example of the class of clergymen by which the Church of England was very much degraded at that period.

Dr. Oliver's history printed the following "Dismissal of the Rev. Thomas Gilpin," from the original document found in the possession of Mr. Neve, of Wolverhampton, in 1836:—

> We, whose names are subscribed, the undoubted and immediate lords of the Manor of Stow Health, hearing and well weighing the said complaints of the Inhabitants of the towne of Willenhall, lying within our said Manor, made and brought against you, Thomas Gilpin, clerk, Curate of the Chapell there:
>
> Doe in consideration thereof and in pursuance of an Order made and inrolled on some of the Rolls of the Court of our said Manor, bearing date 11th day of October in the Sixth Year of the Reign of our late Soveraigne, Lord, King James, over England, etc.
>
> And of our power and authority thereby, Displace and Discharge you, the said Thomas Gilpin, from the place, Dignity, and office of Curate, Minister, or Priest in the said Chapell.
>
> And do hereby present and allow John Carter, clerk (a person elected and approved by the Inhabitants of Willenhall aforesaid), to be Curate of the said Chapell in your place and stead, to read divine service there; and to do and perform all such other offices and things as shall properly belong to his Ministerial function and calling.
>
> And thus much you, the said Thomas Gilpin, are hereby desired to take notice of.
>
> Dated under our hands and seals this 18th day of November in the year of our Lord God, 1674, and in the six-and-twentieth year of the reigne of our Soveraigne Lord, Charles II., by the grace of God, King of England, etc.
>
> Walter Giffard. L.S.
>
> W. Leveson Gower. L.S.

After the expulsion of Mr. Gilpin the Rev. John Carter, who was appointed to succeed him, continued in the Curacy of Willenhall till his death in

1722. In 1727 mention is made of a Mr. Holbrooke being Curate of Willenhall.

Soon after the Registers assist in tracing the successive holders of the benefice. Here are three interesting memoranda, for instance, bearing the signature of the Rev. Titus Neve:—

> 1748, March 4th.—The faculty for rebuilding and enlarging ye chapel of Willenhall, ye then present minister, ye Rev. Titus Neve—(to charge and receive certain fees, etc.)
>
> 1750, January 20.—Then it was yt service began to be performed in ye New Chapel, after almost two years discontinuance, by Titus Neve, Curate.
>
> 1763, February 17th.—Joyce Hill made oath that ye body of Benjamin Stokes was buried in a shroud of Sheep's Wool only, pursuant to an Act of Parliament in that case made and provided.—Witness my hand,
>
> Titus Neve.

(This entry has reference to the Act for Burying in Woollen, one of those pieces of legislative folly whereby it was sought to bolster up artificially our decaying trade in wool.)

The Rev. Titus Neve, whose descendants at the present day are a well-known Wolverhampton family, was born at Much Birch in Herefordshire, son of the Rev. Thomas Neve, in 1717. He matriculated at Balliol College, Oxford, became Rector of Darlaston, 1764, holding the two livings, together with the Prebendary of Hilton his death in 1788. He was buried at Willenhall.

A sermon preached by him in Worcester Cathedral on August 12th, 1762, was printed in Birmingham by the celebrated Baskerville (see Simms' "Bibliotheca Staffordiensis").

His successor was the Rev. William Moreton, who, according to an entry in the Registers, was "sequestered to the vacant chapelry of Willenhall, December 4th, 1788." Toward the close of his ministry Mr. Neve appears to have had the assistance of Curates—George Lewis signs the Registers as "Clerk, Curate" between December, 1778, and July, 1779; and the signature of Mr. Moreton in the same capacity begins to appear in 1784. Among the entries of the last-named is a record that in 1786 he paid the "tax" on a number of Baptisms and Burials himself, whereas in 1785 he shows that a "Collector" received it.

* * * * *

The advent of the Rev. W. Moreton marks an epoch, and we now turn aside to consider the peculiar history of the Advowson, or right of presentation to the living of Willenhall. In 1409 it is found in private hands, being then the property of William Bushbury and his wife (see Chapter VII.).

When the lord of a manor built a church on his own demesne, he often appointed the tithes of the manor to be paid to the officiating minister there, which before had been given to the clergy in common; the lord who thus founded the church often endowed it with glebe, and retained the power of nominating the minister (canonically qualified) to officiate therein. But a chapel-of-ease like Willenhall, built by a resident in the locality, often had its minister, maintained by the subscriptions of persons living close around it, and they naturally claimed to elect their own ministers. The authorities at the mother church would reserve the right to approve and confirm, and would see that they suffered no loss of fees and other emoluments.

An old book in the Registry at Windsor (without date) contains this entry:—

> The curacy of Willenhall is endowed with land to the value of £35. The lords of Stow Heath have, in the last two vacancies, usurped upon the Dean and Chapter, and have nominated to it.

Shaw, the county historian, writing in 1798, after stating that whoever holds the Curacy of Willenhall must have a licence from the Dean of Wolverhampton, proceeds to say:—

> There has been lately a serious contest between the Marquis of Stafford and the inhabitants about the nomination of a curate.

> The gift of the living (says the same authority), or nomination of the minister or curate, is in the principal inhabitants that have lands of inheritance here. He is to be approved of by the lords of the manor, and admonished by them when he does amiss; and if he does not amend in half a year, they may turn him out and nominate another.

This practice is believed to have existed in Willenhall since the time of James I.

The power of the parishioners to elect their own clergymen, though not common, exists in various parts of the country; as at Hayfield and Chapel-in-le-Frith, both in Derbyshire; and in this more immediate locality at St. John's Deritend, Birmingham, and at Bilston and Bloxwich, nearer still.

In London the only example where the elective principle is employed in the choice of a parish priest is presented by Clerkenwell. But wheresoever a vacancy of the kind has to be filled by popular election, with all the accessories incidental to the turmoil of Parliamentary electioneering, all the bitterness of party strife, the parish is inevitably divided into two or more factions; while the clergyman upon whom the lot eventually falls must for a long time afterwards be regarded as the nominee of one of them, rather than the spiritual director of the whole body of the people. He succeeds to his high office as a victor in a great parochial struggle which cannot fail to leave behind it those feelings of rancour so harmful in matters sacred.

The only remedy for this state of things seems to be the voluntary surrender of their privilege by the parishioners; or the provisions of a special Act of Parliament.

As to the soundness of the general principle of a people being consulted in the choice of their spiritual pastor, there can scarcely be two opinions. But where the danger lurks in a case like that of Willenhall is the assumption of our English law—an assumption quite unwarranted in any country where freedom of conscience exists, and with us one of the penalties for maintaining an established State Church—that every parishioner is a Churchman.

Now, as a matter of fact, votes are recorded at these elections by Romanists, by Dissenters of various shades of opinion, by those who are unattached to any religious denomination, and by many who never, at other times, take a great interest in Church of England affairs. At the last election even trustees of Nonconformist chapels were empowered to vote if they were householders, and the trust in respect of which they qualified had been constituted by a properly executed deed. So it can scarcely be claimed that the choice of minister rests solely with those most concerned, namely, the congregation, the customary worshippers at St. Giles's Church.

Resuming the story of the benefice at the election of 1788, it is said that Mr. Moreton having been elected, the then lords of the manor declined to present him to the bishop on the ground that they did not regard him as a fit and proper person. Litigation ensued, and the High Court of Justice declared the election void, and ordered a new one. Meanwhile, the income seems to have sequestrated, probably lying in the hands of the churchwardens till the new minister should be properly instituted.

The electors for a second time returned Moreton, and the lords of the manor then took up the attitude that it was not part of their duty to live in litigation, either with the electors or with Moreton; they had expressed their opinion of the man in the strongest manner possible, and this they considered relieved them from further responsibility; so now at the electors' wish they nominated him to the bishop for induction, and in due course he was formally inducted.

The new incumbent of Willenhall was popularly given out to be an illegitimate "nephew" of George III.; he bore a strong facial likeness to the Royal family, and had been at college with the Duke of York. But whatever his origin or extraction, he was a typical sporting parson of the old school, an enthusiastic cock-fighter, and "a three-bottle man."

It was not long before the old mocking doggerel was applied to Willenhall:—

> A tumble-down church—
> A tottering steeple—
> A drunken parson—
> And a wicked people!

That this old rhyme fairly described the condition of things we may venture to believe if we can also accept as true the rhyme oft quoted by this Willenhall worthy, and which was said to embody his philosophy:—

> Let back and sides and head go bare,
>   Let foot and hand go cold,
> But God send belly good ale enough,
>   Whether it be new or old.

Of "Parson Moreton" innumerable tales are told, all of them racy, though not a few of them apochryphal. There can be little doubt that in the later years of his life he was a bon vivant, and indulged openly in the less refined sports of the period, a cockfight above all things having a strong fascination for him.

And yet, on the plea that "a merciful man is good to his beast," he indulged his old grey pony, "Bob," on which he regularly ambled about, with a share of every tankard of ale he quaffed on his rounds, till the knowing quadruped refused to pass any inn along the road for miles around without stopping for refreshment.

Parson Moreton is not to be judged by modern standards. At that time the church was asleep; and Dr. Johnson once declared that he did not know one religious clergyman. Though the Parson of Willenhall became noted throughout the countryside for his eccentricities, he managed to labour among the rough population, to whom he ministered, with some sort of success.

Into all his lapses from the conventionalities of clericalism, he was a gentleman at the core, having a dignified bearing and a commanding presence. He candidly admitted his shortcomings as a clergyman, telling his flock to do as he said, not as he did. This naturally failed to satisfy very many of them; and it has been asserted that the strength of Dissent in Willenhall at the present time is directly due to the influence of his incumbency.

Of the Rev W. Moreton, it may at least be said that he was a remarkably fine reader, and his sermons were always well-constructed compositions. For many years he lived with Mr. Isaac Hartill in the house at the corner of the Market Place, opposite the Metropolitan Bank; an old house still retaining its original oak floors and staircase, and its substantial old-fashioned doors of the same material, although the building is now made into two shops.

For nearly fifty years Parson Moreton was a familiar figure in the streets of Willenhall. His last signature in the Registers appears in 1833, a year previous to which the Rev. George Hutchinson Fisher had come into the parish to assist him, taking up his residence in the house next to "The Neptune Inn," now the Police Station. He died July 16th, 1834, and was buried on Sunday the 20th.

When Mr. Fisher came to preach Mr. Moreton's funeral sermon, the most notable feature of the oration was the absence of direct reference to the departed. Towards the close of the sermon, however, the following passage was uttered with impressive solemnity:—

> "May every occasion like the present bring instruction and edification to your souls. May the failings which you have witnessed and lamented in others urge you to examine and correct your own; and when their removal makes you think on the nature of the account they will have to render, may you be awakened to scrutinise your own stewardship; and instead of recording the sins of the departed, seek to be delivered, whilst the Redeemer invites you, from those which are a burden to your consciences."

Truly a charitable and Christian-like obituary!

XIX.—How a Flock Chose its own Shepherd.

The living of St. Giles's, Willenhall, popularly supposed to be worth some fourteen hundred pounds a year, the reversion of it was looked upon with eager eyes by not a few of the surrounding clergy. Between Darlaston and Willenhall, particularly, there seems to have existed some sort of pretensions to a clerical inter-relationship.

The Rev. Titus Neve, who held the living of Willenhall from about 1748 to 1788, acted as Curate of Darlaston in 1760, and became Rector of that parish in 1764; while his son, the Rev. Charles Neve, was also Curate there from 1790 to 1793. The Willenhall record of his ministry and interment runs:—

> The Revd. Titus Neve, Minister, Curate, or Stipendiary Priest of Willenhall Chapelry, Prebendary of Hilton and Sacrist of the Collegiate Church of Wolverhampton, and Rector of Darlaston, in the County of Stafford, departed this life December 23rd, 1788, and was interred in the Chancel.

His successor, the Rev. William Moreton, went as Curate to Darlaston in 1786, and was sequestered to the vacant chapelry of Willenhall, December 24th, 1788, the day following Mr. Neve's decease.

At the termination of Mr. Moreton's tenure, the Rev. George William White, who had been a curate at Darlaston from 1823, made a very determined bid for the Incumbency of Willenhall; and although, as we shall see, he was not successful, he was able to console himself, some nine years later, with the rectory of Darlaston (1843).

It appeared that when the Rev. W. Moreton became very old he neglected his duties sadly, often keeping funerals and congregations waiting an unconscionable time, greatly to the scandal of the whole parish. In consequence of this the Churchwardens induced the Incumbent, two or three years before his death, to appoint and pay an energetic young Curate to assist him in his parochial ministrations.

The Curate appointed under these circumstances, as already mentioned, was the Rev. G. H. Fisher, who speedily became a favourite, and by most Willenhall people came to be looked upon as the only possible successor to Mr. Moreton.

Long before the advent of Mr. Fisher, however, the Darlaston folk had settled in their own minds that their Rector, the Rev. Mr. White, was to annex the Willenhall living whenever it become vacant. Whether they looked upon it as being appurtenant to the more important office of their own shepherding cannot be determined at this distance of time; but certain it is that an intense feeling of rivalry existed between the men of Darlaston and the men of Willenhall. The intensity of the feeling may best be judged by a remarkable incident which occurred some five years before Mr. Fisher appeared on the scene.

During the earlier months of the year 1827 it would appear that there had been, from time to time, incursions and alarms between the two towns, and even rioting that involved hand to hand fighting in the streets. Never were such exciting times in these places. At last the rivalry culminated in an act of aggression as daring in execution as it was original in conception—the Willenhall men woke up one fine Sunday morning to find that the Darlastonians had entered their town in the dead of night and stolen the cock from the church steeple!

Now the desperate achievement of this triumph over their enemies had a deeper significance than at first meets the eye. It must be borne in the mind that those were the old cockfighting days, when town matched against town their gamest birds, and sought the glories of a victory in the cock-pit. As between these two neighbouring parishes in particular, there had been much vaunting of birds and challenging to the arbitrament of the spur; the Darlaston men would take a game cock into Willenhall, hold him up to show him the weathercock on the steeple, and then give vent to a roar of defiant laughter when the bird crowed his challenge.

By way of reprisal the men of Willenhall would raid Darlaston, and pretend to call the cock from the steeple there by scattering corn in the churchyard, in mocking allusion to an old tale of Darlastonian simplicity. No wonder, therefore, that the ridiculed were at last exasperated beyond endurance, and that the coup de main of stealing the Willenhall cock was not only projected, but carried to its marvellously successful issue.

Consternation reigned supreme in Willenhall; it was felt that the pass to which matters had been brought by the enormity of this latest aggravation by their enemies could only be met by an appeal to the law, which, hitherto, both factions had so recklessly set at naught. So the following public notice was promptly issued:—

> 10 GUINEAS REWARD.
>
> Whereas, early on Sunday morning last, some evil disposed Persons did steal and carry away the
>
> WEATHERCOCK
> from off the
> STEEPLE.

Any Person giving Information so that the Offenders may be apprehended, shall upon Conviction receive TEN GUINEAS REWARD over and above what is allowed by the Association for the prosecution of Felons. And as more than one were concerned, if either will impeach his Accomplice or Accomplices, they shall receive the above Reward, and every endeavour used to obtain a free Pardon.

Willenhall,
  July 24, 1827.

THOMAS HINCKS,
JAMES WHITEHOUSE,

Chapel Wardens.

    Bassford, Printer, Bilston.

The Notice proved totally unproductive of results, for no Darlaston man was found mean enough to betray the heroes of this daring escapade. Therefore, as the trophy of Darlastonian valour could not be recovered, and St. Giles's tower could not be left in all its nakedness without being an ever-present reproach to the Willenhallers, a new vane had forthwith to be provided for the church.

It was some time after the Willenhall pride had been thus lowered that the old weathercock was accidentally found by some miners who were re-opening an old coal pit which lay between the rival townships. Almost needless to say, the new vane was instantly fetched down, and the old one once more set up to flaunt itself as bravely as of yore in the eyes of distant Darlaston.

The good folk of Willenhall, feeling humiliated, did all in their power to cover up their shame by burying the episode in oblivion; and to this day Willenhall men will deny that the Darlastonians ever came and took away their church weathercock. By way of throwing doubt upon the historical accuracy of the incident, they point to the fact that the church at that time had no spire; it is known, however, that a vane surmounted the church tower, and there is evidence of the Reward Notice, the loose wording of which is responsible for the use of the term "steeple" to signify a tower.

The authenticity of the said Notice is always open to investigation, for a framed copy of it still hangs in the Neptune Inn, preserved as a curiosity. (This copy, probably the only one in existence, bears intrinsic evidence of being a genuine document, and is a treasured possession of the Baker family, to whom the "Neptune" property belonged, the paper having been discovered some fifty years ago in a piece of old furniture, by Mr. Phillips, a connection of his family.)

Resuming the history of the benefice, it may be observed that a doubt has been raised whether Mr. Moreton had to go through a contested election in 1788, but there can be no doubt as to an electoral struggle in 1834. Mr. Fisher soon found himself drawn into the vortex of factional strife, for he was speedily pounced upon by the home party, and very much against his will adopted as their figure-head, if not their champion.

When, on the death of Mr. Moreton, the period of Election came within measurable distance, the excitement became more intense; the patriotic supporters of Mr. White invading the Willenhall territory day after day. Such challenging and fighting, such threatenings and retaliations, surely never were known; one faction had no sooner hurled its defiance at the other than both incontinently plunged headlong into the melée, and rioting once more raged fiercely through the public streets.

Cracked sconces, broken noses, split ears and black eyes resulted by the score; to which list of casualties must be added the number of the half-drowned who had to be rescued from the canal. Onslaughts made on public-houses and other party headquarters led to a considerable destruction of property, which, however, was borne with much complacency when it was remembered that the whole Hundred would be called upon to pay the bill.

Among the candidates for the Incumbency were the Rev. R. Robinson, lecturer at the Collegiate Church, Wolverhampton, in recommendation of whom Mr. G. B. Thorneycroft wrote a letter, dating it from Chapel House in that town, 16 July, 1834; the Rev. John Howells, the Rev. Mr. Rogers, the Rev. Mr. Gwyther, and the Rev. Mr. Wenman; but the Rev. George Hutchinson Fisher, who had been Curate two and a-half years in the town, was recognised as the most formidable competitor. He was the son of a headmaster of Wolverhampton Grammar School, and an M.A. (1834) of Christ College, Cambridge. He received his nomination from Mr. Jeremiah Hartill, and there was little doubt of his ability to obtain the necessary approval of the lords of the manor and the confirmatory licence of the Dean of Wolverhampton.

At that time the Duke of Cleveland was impropriator, but the tithes had been leased by his Grace to Messrs. James Whitehouse and Charles Quinton.

As the day of battle approached public feeling ran so high that on the eve of the poll, which took place on August 5th and 6th, 1834, the Returning Officer deemed it prudent to issue the following Appeal to the Inhabitants:—

It is represented to me, from numerous quarters, that the excitement of the approaching Nomination of a Minister to your Chapel renders it imprudent to take the Poll at the time and place appointed.

Gentlemen,—I cannot but hope and believe that such fears are unnecessary; and, relying upon your good sense, I have determined not to make any alteration in the present arrangements.

I have no interest in your choice; it is my duty only to act with impartiality between all parties.

For that purpose I shall be at your Church at Ten O'clock To-morrow Morning, but unless every person entitled to vote has free and Unmolested Access to the Poll, I shall, of course, be under the NECESSITY of adjourning it.

I address myself to the friends of Each Candidate Alike, and entreating you to allow the proceedings of the day to take place with that moderation which their object and the sacred place in which we shall meet so particularly require.

I am, Gentlemen,
Your faithful, humble Servant,

FRANCIS HOLYOAKE.

Tettenhall, August 4, 1834.

Needless to say, all this rowdyism and disgraceful violence were sternly reprobated by Mr. Fisher, whose rabid opponents must have come to realise that their cause was a lost one when they waylaid the polling clerk and tore his poll-book to shreds.

As to the Magistrates and the Constables, the custodians of the peace discreetly pursued a policy of the most masterly inactivity. Perhaps they felt that the resources of their command were totally inadequate to cope with an uprising of the dimensions and intensity which presented themselves to their consideration; or, maybe, they philosophically recognised that these stirring tumults were the inevitable concomitants of a parochial struggle of so momentous a character. Anyway, their attitude appears to have been justified when everything settled down quietly after the election, the Fisheries tranquilised by victory, and the White Boys dejected by defeat.

For the voting resulted easily in favour of Mr. Fisher, though the validity of his return was challenged in the Court of Chancery for some three years afterwards, during which time, however, he had no hesitation in officiating. He was a fine reader and an able speaker, his delivery of the Church ritual being a model of correct elocution.

Like his predecessor, he held the living a long time, the tenure of the two covering a century. Mr. Fisher resided for a number of years at Bentley Hall.

In 1887, soon after Mr. Fisher's "Jubilee" in Willenhall, a public movement was instituted, in which many Dissenters took part, to acknowledge his fifty years of devoted service among all classes of the community. A presentation was made to him of a silver service and his portrait in oils—the latter the work of Thomas Hill, a native of Wednesfield, and which now hangs on the walls of the Free Public Library.

XX.—The Election of 1894, and Since.

Although St. Giles's Church is known as the Parish Church, and a church has probably been on the same site some six centuries, the church of Willenhall is really a Proprietary Chapel of Ease, and its Incumbent legally nothing more than a Perpetual Curate, or Curate in Charge, though Incumbent of Willenhall, and receiving in respect of that office a very substantial "living." The official return set forth in Crockford's Clergy Directory for 1893 was: Tithe rent charge, £640, net Income, £1,300.

Strictly, there is no St. Giles's parish, nor any parish attached to St. Giles's Church, and in law the Incumbent might, if he wished, ignore the so-called parish so long as he performed satisfactorily certain duties in the church. The unappropriated district, commonly known as St. Giles's parish, includes that part of Willenhall which has not been allocated to the properly constituted parishes (or ecclesiastical districts) of St. Stephen's, St. Anne's, and Holy Trinity, Short Heath, plus the entire civil parish of Bentley—the whole being really part of the ecclesiastical parish of Wolverhampton.

The position is extraordinarily anomalous. The Incumbent is elected by the inhabitants of the township of Willenhall being sufficient householders and having lands of inheritance there; that is to say, the voters must be freeholders as well as householders. Litigation followed the choice of the Rev. William Moreton in 1788, and also the election of the Rev. G. H. Fisher in 1834. It is understood that this system of "patronage" has been condemned by the Privy Council; and that application has been made for the proper constitution of a St. Giles's parish, but the Bishop demands a quid pro quo.

All attempts to create a Parish of Willenhall have, so far, utterly failed. The existing system of patronage is always the obstacle, and nothing will induce the voters either to sell or to surrender their rights in the Advowson.

To fully realise the position it must be borne in mind that in addition to the three constituted "parishes" created within the original township of Willenhall since Mr. Fisher became Incumbent of Willenhall in 1834, Short Heath is now a separate township, with separate District Council, and that Bentley has its Rural District Council—so that persons who live in Bentley parish, Short Heath parish, the three constituted ecclesiastical district parishes or districts, and the unappropriated remainder of the township (nominally St. Giles's parish), have all the right to vote for the clergyman if they have the necessary other qualifications of householder and freeholder.

On the death of the Rev. G. H. Fisher in 1894, no less than 23 formal applications were forthcoming for the vacant living. The keynote was given at a preliminary meeting of St. Giles's congregation, at which Dr. J. T. Hartill presided, and when the most likely candidates were formally proposed and seconded for adoption.

The voting (recorded on cards) resulted in favour of the Rev. William Elitto Rosedale, M.A., Rector of Canton, Cardiff, for whom there were 265, as against 26 given for the Rev. W. L. Ward, of St. Anne's, Willenhall. The Churchwardens consistently directed the procedure at this public election as nearly as possible along the lines which would be followed by private patronage; they declined to take any active part in the circulation of testimonials, or afford facilities for any candidate to preach in the church, to the possible prejudice of the others, but they passively acquiesced in each one approaching the electors in any way which seemed fitting and proper to himself.

The votes recorded on this occasion were:—

Rev. W. E. Rosedale (Canton, Cardiff)	199
Rev. W. L. Ward (St. Anne's, Willenhall)	157
Rev. J. E. Page (Binfield)	28
Rev. F. W. Ford (London)	1

At four o'clock, Mr. Page (who was the son of a local iron-master) and Mr. Ford retired in favour of Mr. Ward. The Returning Officer was Mr. R. N. Hearne, Steward to the Lords of the Manor of Stowheath, the Duke of Sutherland and Mr. W. T. C. Giffard; and the poll was taken by open voting, each voter recording his vote orally and within the hearing of all present.

The result having been forwarded to the Lords of the Manor, they formally nominated the one at the head of the poll to the Bishop for appointment and induction to the living. The successful candidate was a native, being the son of the Rev. D. Rosedale, to whose exertions the building of Holy Trinity Church was largely due, and in the Vicarage House attached to which the said candidate was born. But he possessed other than local claims, though these, no doubt, prepossessed many Willenhall folk in his favour.

There can be little doubt the election of 1894 was conducted with far more tact and discretion than ever had been exercised on similar occasions previously. There was still the old risk of serious public disturbances; but perhaps more than ever there was, as must generally be the case in such methods of conducting a controversial matter of this description, the danger of unseemly and acrimonious squabblings in public. It reflects the highest credit upon the Churchwardens and all others concerned in the election, that not only was nearly all this avoided, but the possibility always present, of long and embittered litigation to follow, was also reduced to a minimum. It required some firmness and decision to weed down 23 formal applications, and more than twice that number of business-like inquiries, to workable limits for taking a poll.

The litigation of 1834 had arisen through the manufacture of "faggot votes," which were eventually disallowed, and had to be struck off. A difficulty arose in 1894 as to the interpretation of an Act of 1844—would Lord Blandford's Act debar from taking part in the voting the residents in the newly-created ecclesiastical districts of St. Stephen's, St. Anne's, and Holy Trinity, Short Heath? Although at first dubious on the question, the authorities answered it in the negative.

* * * * *

As previously stated, the earliest record of the Advowson is of the year 1408. In the Salt Collections, Vol. XI., p. 218, we find that by a final concord recorded "on the morrow of St. Martin, 10 Henry IV., William Bysshebury and Joan, his wife, acknowledged that seven messuages, eight tofts, one mill, sixty acres of land, ten acres of meadow, and 24s. 6½d. of rent in Wolverhampton, and the Advowson of the Chapel of Willenhall to be the right of Richard Hethe and William Prestewood, chaplain, and the latter granted them to William Bysshebury and Joan for their lives, with remainder to John Hampton, of Stourton, and Harvise, his wife, and to the heirs of John for ever."

Exactly two centuries later, as we shall learn in the next chapter, the endowments of, and the right of presentation to, the living were placed upon a definite and legal foundation. Suffice it here to say that at the present time there are Trustees appointed by the Charity Commissioners for the purpose of holding the Trust property belonging to the said living, and, with the assistance of an official representing the Commissioners, managing affairs connected therewith.

The Trust, to which Mr. Samuel Mills Slater is solicitor, is under the full control of the Charity Commissioners, who have to be regularly supplied with certified copies of all the Trust accounts.

As we shall see presently, the original Feoffees of the Trust property were appointed in 1608 by a Commission of local magnates and landowners, consisting of William Overton, Bishop of Lichfield; William, Lord Paget, of Beaudesert; Sir John Bowes, of Elford; Sir Edward Littleton, of Pillaton Hall; Sir Edward Leigh, of Rushall; Sir Simon Weston, of St. John's, Lichfield; Sir Robert Stanford, of Perry Hall; Sir Walter Chetwynde, of Grendon and Ingestre; Sir William Chetwynde, of Grendon (half-brother of Sir Walter); Zachary Babington, Doctor in the Civil Law; Raphe Snead, of Keele; Walter

Bagott, of Blythfield; William Skeffington, of Fisherwick; Roger Fowke, of Brewood and Wyrley; John Chetwynde, of Rudge, parish of Standon, and Walter Stanley, of West Bromwich—most of them justices for the county of Stafford.

By virtue of a provision in the Decree or award of these Commissioners, the surviving Feoffees were enabled to appoint new Feoffees in the places of the deceased ones. In later times, however, by virtue of the Charitable Trusts Acts, the Board of Charity Commissioners acquired the power of making appointments of new Trustees, and also of removing Trustees.

In the year 1889, the number of Trustees had become reduced to one—Mr. John Davies, then residing at Warwick. By an Order dated 23rd July, 1889, the Board removed Mr. Davies, at his own request, from the office of Trustee, and appointed the following gentlemen to be new Trustees:—

John Clark.

Wm. Henry Hartill.

John Thomas Hartill.

Joseph Johnson.

David Wm. Lees.

Jas. Carpenter Tildesley.

Henry Vaughan.

Henry Hartill Walker, junr.

Of these gentlemen only Messrs. J. T. Hartill, Vaughan, and Walker are now living.

It might be necessary under certain conditions (as, for instance, in any action connected with the sale of the Advowson) to constitute a body of elected Trustees (as distinct from the aforementioned nominated Trustees) of not more than eleven, nor less than five members, duly elected at a statutory meeting of the town's inhabitant freeholders.

As a matter of fact, a public meeting of the owners of the Advowson, convened on the requisition of a memorial to the Incumbent (Rev. W. E. Rosedale), signed by a number of them, was held in the month of June, 1900, to consider a proposal for the sale of the said Advowson. A similar proposal had been discussed in 1898 at a public meeting attended by some 200 owners, when it was suggested that half the sum realised should be handed over to the town authorities, while the other half should be spent on the church and schools.

At this second meeting, over which Mr. T. Nicholls, chairman of the District Council, presided, the sale value of the Advowson was variously estimated at sums ranging from £1,100 to £3,000. The minister's income was stated by one speaker to be £539 per annum nett—£508 derived from a sum of £20,974 13s. 11d. invested in Consols, and with other sources making a gross revenue of £641 18s. 9d., from which deductions amounting to £102 7s. 6d. had to be made.

Another speaker gravely cautioned the meeting against over-estimating the capitalised value of this living by remarking that the present incumbent was then a comparatively young man of only forty-two, and healthy at that.

It was given as the opinion of another speaker that the existing method of electing their parson was undesirable in the best interests of the church, and ought to be forthwith discontinued. Also it was contended that if a sale could be effected, any sum that resulted therefrom might very advantageously be expended in the town for the benefit of the inhabitants generally.

One stalwart stickler for "the eternal fitness of things" upheld the sound principle of the members of every church exercising the right to choose their own minister, and he deprecated generally the practice of trafficking in advowsons.

In the end, although those in favour of selling almost threatened to apply for an Act of Parliament for effecting a sale compulsorily, the meeting finally resolved by a very substantial majority: "That it was not advisable at the present time to sell the Advowson."

So that two well-conducted public meetings, held within a brief space of each other, were unable to come to any definite decision by which the position of things would be materially altered.

XXI.—Willenhall Church Endowments.

By the courtesy of Mr. S. M. Slater, of Darlaston, a summarised, but fairly comprehensive account of the Willenhall endowments, and the somewhat exceptional parochial privileges connected therewith, may be given here.

The foundation of the Endowment of the Benefice and the establishment of the right of the Parishioners, or rather the Parishioners of the Township "having lands of inheritance there," may be said to rest upon, or at all events to have been defined and regulated by, three documents, namely:—

(a) A Decree dated the 27th March in the 5th Year of James the 1st (1607), made in pursuance of an Inquisition, or Commission, issued by the King on the 12th February of the previous (regnal) year.

(b) A Deed of the 23rd September of the 6th Year of James the 1st (1608), entered into between the Lords of the Manor of Stowheath on the one hand, and Sir Walter Levison and others, on behalf of themselves and the rest of the Inhabitants of Willenhall, on the other hand.

(c) A Memorandum entered on the Court Rolls of the Manor of Stowheath, dated the 10th October in the 6th Year of James the First (1608).

Reference to Chapter VII. of this work will recall how a Chantry Chapel had been founded and endowed in Willenhall by the Gerveyse family. This Chantry Chapel would be a "separated place" within the Chapel-of-Ease specially used to celebrate masses for the departed souls of certain persons. Now, one of the earliest signs of the approaching Reformation was a decline in the belief in Purgatory; and presently Henry VIII. was empowered by Act of Parliament to seize all lands, tenements, rents, &c., which had been given for the maintenance of Chantry Priests, with all their lamps, candles, torches, and other expensive appointments for what were declared to be "superstitious" uses. But a right was reserved to the King, as head of the Church, to direct such properties to uses which could be regarded as truly "charitable." What became of the Willenhall Chantry endowments?

It is the opinion of Mr. A. A. Rollason, no mean authority on the subject— vide his recondite articles in the "Dudleian," having special reference to a similar Commission of Inquiry held in 1638 as to the alienation of lands belonging to Dudley Grammar School—that the Willenhall Inquisition, or Commission of Inquiry, was brought about, as was that at Dudley, in consequence of the uncertain state of the law as to whether the lands, and the income therefrom, came within the Charitable Uses Act; or whether the gifts were absolutely void.

For while Magna Charta declared "that if any one shall give lands to a religious house, the grant shall be void, and the land forfeited to the lord of the fee"—the abbots of old took care to be "lords of the fee," usually holding their lands direct from the King—there was a Statute of Edward III. by which the King was empowered to grant a Royal licence affording relaxation of lands held under the Statutes of Mortmain.

It seems almost impossible to doubt that the freehold lands belonging to the Willenhall Chantry had escaped confiscation to the Crown under the Statute, I Edward VI., if they had been held solely for performing obits and singing masses for the dead. Yet it is just possible they may have been re-granted to aid in the maintenance of the Curate of the Chapel-of-Ease, in which case they would be recognised as a "charitable use," and were consequently safe.

The Willenhall Inquisition of 1607 was addressed by the King (as stated in the last chapter) to "The Reverend Father in God, William, Bishopp of Coventrie and Lichfield And to our right trustie and well beloved William Lord Pagett and to our trustie and well beloved Sir John Bowes, Sir Edward Littleton, Sir Edward Leigh, Sir Simon Weston, Sir Robert Stanford, Sir Walter Chetwynde and Sir William Chetwynde, Knights, Zacharie Baington (Babington), Doctor of Lawe, Chancellor of Lichfield, Raphe Sneade, Walter Bagott, William Skevington (Skeffington), Roger Fowke, John Chetwynde, and Walter Stanley, Esquires."

It set forth that the King, for the due execution of a certain Statute of 43 Queen Elizabeth, intituled an Act to "redress the misimployment of landes goods and stocks of money theretofore given to charitable uses," and having special trust and confidence in their approved fidelities, &c., had appointed the persons named "to be our Commissions," and thereby gave to them and to any four or more of them full power and authority to enquire "as well by the Oathes of twelve lawful men or more of the County of Stafford as by all other good and lawful waies and meanes accordinge to the purporte and true meaninge of the said Statute, What landes, etc., have at any tyme or tymes been given by us or any of our progenitors or by any other well disposed pson or psons, bodies politique or corporate, for the reliefe of aged impotent and poore people etc.—And of all and singular the abuses misdemeanors breaches of trusts negligences misimployments notimployinge, concealinge, defraudinge, misconvertinge or misgovernment of the same landes tenements rents anuyties pffits hereditments goods chattels money or stocks of money or any of them heretofore given lymitted appointed or assigned to or for any charitable and godlie uses before rehearsed accordinge to the purporte and true meaninge of the said Statute. And upon such enquirie hearinge and examyninge thereof accordinge to the said Statute to sett downe such Orders Judgments and Decrees as the said landes tenements rents anuyties pffits hereditaments goods chattels money and stocks of money may be dulie and faithfullie employed to and for such of the charitable uses and intents before rehearsed respectively for which they were given limited assigned or appointed by the donors and founders thereof accordinge to the purporte and true meaninge of the said Statute."

The Commission then proceeds:—

> And therefore we commande you that at cteyne days and places which you or any foure or more of you shall appoint in this behalf ye or any foure or more of you doe make diligent Inquirie and Inquiries upon the pmisses and all and singuler the same and all other things appointed by the said Statute for you or any foure or more of you to doe and execute that ye or foure of you at the least pforme doe and execute that effecte in all points and in everie respect accordinge to the said Statute.... And the same Inquisicon and Inquisicons and everie of them togeather with all decrees Judgments orders and proceedinges which you or any foure or more of you shall accordinge to the said Statute thereupon make or sett downe that you or foure or more of you have before Us in our Chancery with all convenient speede . . . under the hands and seals of any foure or more of you. . . And we also command by authoritie hereof our Sheriffe of our said County of Stafford that at such times dayes and places as you or any foure or more of you shall appoint to him he shall cause to come before you or any foure or more of you such and as many honest and lawful men of the said County as well within the liberties as without by whom the truth in the pmisses may best be known to inquire of the pmisses upon their Oathes as you or any foure or more of you shall require and command him.

The Decree before referred to was signed by Sir Edward Leigh, Dr. Zacharie Babington, William Skeffington, John Chetwynde, and Walter Stanley, and was addressed to the Right Honourable Thomas, Lord Ellesmere, Lord Chancellor of England. It set out the Commission and then proceeded as follows:—

> Wee therefore by verteue of the said Commission dyd award a pcept to the Sheriffe of the said Countye to somon foure and twentye good and lawfull men of his Baylywicke to be before Us at Lichfeilde the xxijth day of Marche laste paste and did also send a precepte to one Jane Lane Widdow and to Thomas Lane Esquire that claymed intereste in the pmisses to bee before Us att the same day and place to sett forth theire and either of theire tytles (yf

they had anie) to the said pmisses att wch daye and place by virtue of the said pcepte to the sayde Sheriffe dyrected as aforesaid a full Jury dyd appeare and Councell on the behalfe of Mrs. Lane and the said Thomas Lane dyd alsoe appear before Us and thereupon wee pceeded to sweare the Jurye who bringe sworne and chardged to inquire of the pmisses after long evidence and examinacon of many witnesses on both pts the said Jurors gave up theire verdicte in such sorte as by an Inquisition hereunto annexed Sealed and subscribed (wch wee doe herewith all ctyfye unto yor Lordshippe into the highe Courte of Chancery) maie appear; that is to say that a pcell of pasture or land called Marchyhills alias Bessalls in Bentley aforesaid, of ye yeerlie value of fyve pounds, was before the fourth yeere of Kinge Edward the Sixth given to Nicholas Hellyn and Richard Whorwood gent., John Podmore Willm Greene Willm Whitmore and William Podmore and their heires to bee Imployed to saye devine service in the Chappell of Willenhall aforesaid for the ease of the Inhabyants there being farre remoote from their prshe Church of Wolverhampton in the said Countye that the pffits of the said lands were from Anno quarto of Kinge Edwarde the sixte so imployed as aforesaid by the space of dyvers yeeres of the said Jane Lane and Thomas Lane and their Tenants And that the same have been misemployed by the space of one whole yeere now laste paste and more all wch pmisses considered wee doe order and decree at Lichfeilde aforesaid by verteue of the said Comission in manner and form followinge That is to saie that the said pcell of groundes and all ye rents revenues yssues and pffitts thereof shall for ever hereafter bee imployed and bestowed upon and towards the maynetaynance of a Curate or Chaplyne for the tyme being to saie devine service in the said Chappell for the ease of the Inhabitants there and that John Wilkes of Willenhall in the said Countye gent, Willm Flemynge als Greene of Willenhall in the said Countye yeoman, Leonard Tomkis of Willenhall in the said Countye yeoman, John Bate of Willenhall in the said Countye yeoman, Richard Bate of Willenhall in the saide Countye yeoman, Willm Baylie of Willenhall in the said Countye yeoman, and Willm Brindley of Willenhall in the said Countye yeoman, theire heires and Assignes shall have and hold the said pmisses to the use and entente aforesaid according to a former feoffm't

> thereof made and shewed forth to the said Jury at the tyme of the same Inquisicon taken and shall from tyme to tyme and at all tymes hereafter yeerelie Imploye and bestowe the full value thereof upon and towards the maynetaynance of a Curate or Chaplyne to saye devyne service in the said Chappell.

As will be seen, the Decree states clearly that the yearly income of the Bentley lands was to be used towards the maintenance of a Curate to say Divine Service in the Chapel; this at once brought it under the Charitable Uses Act, and removed it from liability to be confiscated under 23, Henry VIII., c. 10., for perpetuating practices regarded as superstitious and contrary to Reformation doctrines. It will be noted that a "former feoffment" is mentioned—may not this have been a re-grant by the King, which has been hinted at? The grant to Nicholas Hellyn and others in 4 Edward VI. has all the appearance of being a gift from the Crown to the purposes of the newly constituted Church of England.

The Decree then proceeds, as mentioned in the last chapter, to make provision for the filling up of vacancies in the number of Feoffees whenever the number may be reduced to three.

It will be noticed that the Inquisition and Decree, as given above, deal only with the title to and the application of the income of certain freehold lands at Bentley. The Deed of the 23rd September of the 6th Year of James the 1st (1608), and the Memorandum of the 10th October of the same year, however, appear to deal with what seems to be the remainder of the endowment of the Curacy, and with the status of the Priest or Curate. The Deed and the Memorandum set forth, in effect, the same set of facts; and the former may be described as the Contract out of Court between the parties interested, and the latter as being the Official Record of the Contract entered upon the Rolls of the Manor. The Deed is stated to be made between the Right Worshipful Sir John Levison, Knight, of Lilleshall, in the County of Salop, and John Giffard, of Chillington, in the County of Stafford, Esquire, on the one part, and Sir Walter Levison, of Wolverhampton, Knight, Thomas Lane, of Bentley, Esquire, Richard Wilkes, and Thomas Tomkis, of Willenhall, Gentlemen, and William Brindley and William Podmore, of Willenhall, Yeomen, on behalf of themselves and the rest of the Inhabitants of Willenhall, on the other part; and after making reference to a "Commission awarded upon the Statute of 43 Elizabeth concerning Lands given to Charitable Uses," it proceeds to state that the lords consent, grant, and decree that the Copyhold lands therein referred to shall be let in the manner and for the purpose therein mentioned, and the effect of such consent, as before pointed out, is recited in the Memorandum entered on the Court Rolls.

Coming to the Memorandum of 1608, it is evident a serious difficulty had arisen with the Willenhall lands held under copyhold tenure, and which were probably dealt with by the same Commission. For there was probably but one Commission of Inquiry, though there may have been two separate Decrees.

Lands held by Copyhold tenure are usually subject to fealty to the Lord of the Manor, and this was doubtless customary in Stowheath. It seems conclusive that the King did not take these lands into his own hands, whereby matters would have been reduced to the absurdity of the lord paramount being called upon to do homage to his own tenant.

The suggestion is offered by Mr. Rollason that the tenure of the lands was not precisely a lay one, but partook of a spiritual nature—was, in fact, not feudal, but what was known as a tenure in frankalmoign or free alms.

The Memorandum commences with a recital as follows:—

> Whereas by a Commission awarded upon a Statute of 43 Elizabeth concerning Lands given to Charitable Uses upon the executinge of wch Comission the Inhabitants and Men of Willenhall in the County of Stafford have made profe that certaine Copyhold Lands in the Towne of Willenhall holden by Coppie of Court Roll of the Manor of Stowheath were formerly Surrendered by certain Feoffees or Stateberers Uppon Trust and confidence that the yearly Pfitts thereof should be imployed for the hyer stipend and wages of a Preist Minister or Curate to say Divine Service in the Chappell of Willenhall from tyme to tyme for ever for the Ease of the Inhabitants there dwelling being two Myles distant from Wolverhampton their Prshe Church and towards the repairinge of the said Chappell and the said yearly pfitts thereof were soe used and imployed for many yeares togeather uppon consideracon of wch said cause and uppon longe debate thereof before divse Comissioners in psence of Councell of both ptes ambiguity and doubtings arisinge whether the said Copyhold Lands were originally given to the maintenance of a Chantery Preist or otherwise to the maintenance of a Curate of Preist to say Divine Service in the Chappell aforesaid The said Inhabitants are contented to refer themselves therein to the consideracon of Sir John Leveson Knt and John Giffard Esquire Lords of the Mannor of Stowheath within wch Mannor the said Towne of Willenhall lyeth and is pcel wch usadge and imploymt of the saide rents and pfitts of the said Lands the

said Sr John Leveson and Jhn Giffard Esqre well accepting of are willing to give furtherance to soe good and charitable an occon And the rather for that their Ancestors have formerly given allowance out of the same Lands for the same purpose And therefore doe for them and their heirs consent and agree that the said Coppyhold Lands shall for ever hereafter be let by the consent of four of the Inhabitants of the said Towne of Willenhall to be chosen by the greater pte of the sufficient Householders of the said Towne having lands of inheritance there, and that the said aforemenconed Lands shall be by the said four Inhabitants let from tyme to tyme according to the trew and reasonable Rate or Valew thereof and the mony pfitts and rents to be reserved out of the said Lands to be imployed half yearly hereafter in manner and forme following (that is to say) First to the payment of eleven shillings yearly for the antient and accustomed cheife rent dew and to be dew to the Lords of the said Manor of Stowheath Secondly to the payment of Six shillings and eight pence yearly towards the reparations of the said Chappell, and thirdly towards the maintenance of a stipendary Preist Minester or Curate for the sayinge of Divine Service Ministeringe of the Holy Sacraments and doinge all such other service in the Chappell of Willenhall as doe and shall belong to his Ministerie and Function wch Stipendary Priest Minister or Curate shall be fro tyme to tyme chosen nominated and appointed by the said Inhabitants of Willenhall for the tyme beinge or the greatest pte of them havinge lands there as aforesaid and prsented and allowed by the Lord on Lords of the said Manner of Stowheath and his and their heir or heires for ever. And it is further ordered that whosoever shall be nominated appointed prsented and allowed as aforesaid to supply the place as Preist Minister or Curate in the said Chappell of Willenhall shall conforme himselfe to the Govermt Eclesiasticall and be resident uppon his cure there, in defalt whereof and uppon complainte made by the said Inhabitants or the greater pte of the sufficient or chiefest of them, eyther of his nonresidence, Insufficiencie, negligence, or any other Misdemenor, to the Lord or Lords of the said Manner for the tyme beinge, yt shall be lawfull for the Lord or Lords of the said Mannor for the tyme beinge to give one halfe yeares warninge to the said Preist Minester or Curate to reform himselfe whch if he doe not then it shall be lawfull for the said Lord or Lords for the tyme beinge to remove and displace him at the end of the said halfe yeare, and to present and allow another Curate Minester or Preist there to be nominated and appointed by the said Inhabitants or the greater part of them as aforesaid. Lastly it is ordered that the said Lands shall at the next Leete at Wolverhampton for the said Mannor of Stowheath be granted by Coppie of Court Roll to Nine Feoffees or Stateberers and their heires then and there to be nominated, uppon wch Grante there shall be Thirteene pounds six shillings and eight pence paid for a Fine and Herriotts, and that after the death of six or seaven of the said Feoffees or Stateberers there shall be sixe or seaven others from tyme to tyme chosen by the said Inhabitants or greatest pte of them to whom and to the other three or two surviving Feoffees and their heires uppon the Surrender of the said three or two Feoffees or Stateberers a new Grant shall be made by Coppie of Court Roll of the said Lands accordinge to the Custome of the said Mannor. And soe from when and as often there shal be remaininge but three or two Feoffees or Stateberers And that uppon every such admittance there shall be payed to the Lords of the said Mannor the some of six pounds thirteen shillings and fower pence for a fine and Herriotts as often as any such admittance shall be as aforesaid.

The disclosure here made, that part of the endowments went to the repair of the church, gives the key to the probable solution; because this unquestionably constituted a "charitable use," and where such was intermixed with a "superstitious use," only so much as went to the latter purpose was subject to confiscation under the reforming Statutes of Henry VIII. A generous interpretation would not inquire too closely into the amount left for a Chantry Priest, and the portion devoted to repairs of the fabric. It was to discriminate between the two kinds of uses that the subsequent Statute of Elizabeth (43 E. Cap. 4) was passed, empowering the Lord Chancellor to appoint Commissions authorised to investigate the complaints of aggrieved parties, and to alter the direction of the endowment funds, where necessary, to make them conformable with the Protestant religion. This was precisely the nature and function of the Willenhall Commission. All it accomplished was done under the authority of the Great Seal of England, the Commissions being generally directed by the Lord Chancellor to the Bishop of the diocese, as in this case; the judgments arrived at, and the decrees issued were given the full force of law. The Willenhall Trust was clearly constituted under this Act of Elizabeth.

On reading the introductory portion of the Memorandum, it will be observed that no date is given to the Commission referred to, which possibly might be interpreted to mean that such Commission was quite separate from the one above set out, inasmuch as the latter related only to freehold land at Bentley, while the Memorandum speaks of "certain Copyhold lands in the Towne of Willenhall" being "surrendered by certain Feoffees . . . Uppon trust," &c.

In the documents before considered no allusion is made to there being any endowment or provision for the maintenance of the Chantry Priest or Curate other than the income from the Freehold and Copyhold lands which respectively formed the subject of those documents; and from this it is reasonable to conclude that such income formed, or was involved in what may be described as practically the only permanent provision for the maintenance of the Incumbent for the time being of the Chapel.

A century ago there appears to have been a prevalent belief that the income of the Incumbent or Curate was about £1,400 per annum. An investigation of what has happened during the last 70 years does not reveal any foundation for the belief. After the election, in the year 1838, of the late Rev. G. H. Fisher to the Curacy, it was considered by him and the Trustees of the Living to be desirable to apply to Parliament for powers to sell the surface of the lands forming the Endowment, or to sell or lease any of the mines thereunder. Accordingly, a private Act of Parliament (7 and 8 Victoria Cap. 19) granting those powers was obtained. The Preamble of this Act refers to dealings with the Copyhold Lands subsequent to the date of the Memorandum before commented upon, there being recitals that, as appears by a surrender dated the 21st November, 1727, certain Copyhold Lands, &c., in the Town of Willenhall were formally surrendered to the use of certain Feoffees and were held upon the trusts already described, and that at a Court Baron held on the 24th September, 1839, the said Copyhold lands were surrendered to the use of Thomas Hinks, John Riley Hinks, John Read, William Stokes, John Mason, Joseph Turner, John Biddle, Jeremiah Hartill and John Davies on the same trusts. The Preamble further shows a small further source of income for the Living, inasmuch as it states that certain Freehold lands in the Township of Willenhall (as well as those in the Township of Bentley) had from time immemorial been held and enjoyed in like manner as the said Copyhold lands and that the said Freehold and Copyhold lands constituted "one and the same Charity." The Preamble further states that there stood in the name of the Accountant-General of the High Court of Chancery the sum of £386 3s. 0d. of three per cent. Consols, and that there was owing from the Birmingham Canal Company a sum of £202 2s. 0d. These two sums represented the agreed prices of lands belonging to the Living taken by the Grand Junction Railway Company and the Canal Company respectively under their compulsory powers. The freehold land in Willenhall before referred to, is comprised (with all the other lands held in Trust for the Living), in the Schedule to the Act, and consisted of a field called Ell Park, containing 1a. 3r. 28p., and produced a rental of £5 12s. 0d.

Touching the supposition before referred to as to the value of the Living being £1,400 per annum, it may be mentioned that the Schedule to the Act gives the total area of the lands held in trust for the Living at 112a. 2r. 37p., and the aggregate amount of the rentals as being £500 15s. 6d. per annum.

A further power sought for and conferred by the Act was the power to raise a sum not exceeding £1,600 to be applied in building a Parsonage House upon any of the land belonging to the Living, or, in the alternative, to purchase at a cost not exceeding £1,600, a Parsonage House, with the consent of the Court of Chancery, if thought more advantageous than to build one.

In the exercise of the powers conferred by the Act, the Trustees, in the course of a few years, sold all the lands belonging to the Living situate in Willenhall, and in recent years a piece of land containing 1 rood and 23 perches, forming part of the Freehold land at Bentley, has also been sold and there now remains at Bentley, belonging to the Living, nine pieces of land, containing a total area of 30 acres and 27 perches, which, for several years prior to Mr. Fisher's death, produced a rental of £20 per annum.

The primary provisions of the Act with regard to the moneys to arise from sales and leases under the powers thereby conferred were: (a) That the moneys should be let out and invested under the direction of the Court in the purchase of Freehold hereditaments or Copyhold hereditaments convenient to be enjoyed therewith; (b) that the premises purchased should be conveyed unto the Trustees for the time being of the Charity and held upon the Trusts, upon which the hereditaments sold would have been held in case the same had not been so sold, and the Act had not been passed; (c) that until the moneys should be so let out and invested they should be invested in Parliamentary stocks or Funds of Great Britain in the name of the Accountant-General; and (d) that the annual produce of such funds should be applied to the person and for the purposes to which the rents of the trust lands would have been applicable.

In the exercise of the trust for purchasing lands conferred by the Act, the Trustees subsequently purchased the property in Walsall Street, adjoining and near to the Churchyard, including the site of the new Schools there, and also two Cottages and some gardens and land at Shepwell Green. The latter property has since been sold off.

Reverting to the question of the value of the Living, it may be mentioned that in the year 1886, when the Shepwell Green property and the small piece of land at Bentley were still in hand, the gross income from the Living, apart from Surplice Fees, was £792 7s. 9d., made up as follows:—

	£	s.	d.
Rents	194	2	8
Dividend from £19,941 16s. 8d., 3 per cent. Consols	598	5	1
	£792	7	9

The effect of the "Goschen" Act of 1888 was ultimately to reduce the Dividend on the Consols by 1/6th, and, consequently, the gross income of the Living, apart from Surplice Fees, stood a few years afterwards at £692 13s. 7d., made up as follows:—

	£	s.	d.
Rents	194	2	8
Dividend from 2½ per cent. Consols	498	10	11
	£692	13	7

This statement brings matters up to date (1907); the tithes are still impropriate, a rent charge of £540 being receivable by Lord Barnard in succession to the Duke of Cleveland. The tithe-owner in Bentley is the Earl of Lichfield.

XXII.—The Church Charities: The Daughter Churches.

At the beginning of the nineteenth century a Royal Commission was appointed to inquire into, and put a stop to, the barefaced robbery of the Church charities, which had been going on for a century or more. Every parish in England was visited, and the Report on the Willenhall Charities was published in 1825 to the following effect:—

1.—PRESTWOOD'S DOLE.

> An ancient Instrument was produced to us, purporting to be a Deed-poll (without any seals thereto, but with a portion of the lower margin torn off, not, however, as it appeared to us, in that part where the seals are usually affixed), bearing date 17 August, 1642, whereby William Prestwood, of Willenhall, in Co. Stafford, and Mariana, his wife, granted to the Wardens and Sidemen of the Church or Chapel of Willenhall, aforesaid, and to the Overseers of the poor of the said Town, and their successors for ever, all the annual rent, profits, and emoluments whatsoever, issuing, renewing, and arising from, in and out of a certain Close of the said William and Mariana, called Canne Byrch, lying and being in Willenhall aforesaid, between Willenhall Field on one part, and the highway leading towards Darlaston on the other; to have and to hold all the rent, profits, and emoluments arising from the said Close, after the death of the said William and Mariana, for ever; to the pious use following, viz.:—
>
> To pay and contribute the annual rent aforesaid to the use and behoof of the Poor in the said Town, at the discretion of the aforesaid Wardens, Officers, and Overseers of the Chapel and Town aforesaid for ever, and not otherwise: And it is further declared that the said rent should be annually paid in the manner and form as the said William by his last Will should appoint.
>
> We have no evidence that this piece of land, which is well known, was ever in the possession of the Parish Officers. It is now considered as the property of Hervey Smith, Esq., of Castle Bromwich, who has lately succeeded to it on the death of his father, the late William Smith, Esq., solicitor of Birmingham, and to be subject only to an annual rent charge of 20s. to the Poor of Willenhall, which is regularly paid by

the tenant of the land. It has been for many years in the possession of Mr. Smith's family, and he produced several receipts, the earliest of which is dated 31 October, 1753, and is for "£1 due Nov. 1st, 1753, for Prestwood's Dole."

The others are for the same sum, designating it either as "Prestwood's Dole," or "A Dole payable to the Poor of Willenhall."

We do not conceive that, under these circumstances, the imperfect Instrument above stated, unaccompanied by possession, can afford any ground to the Parishioners of the Township to claim anything more than the Dole which has been so long paid. The 20 shillings are given away to 20 Poor Widows on St. Thomas's Day.

2.—PEDLEY'S CHARITY.

James Pedley, otherwise Fletcher, by his Will dated 20 May, 1728, after the death of his wife, gave to his brother, Richard Pedley, alias Fletcher, his heirs and assigns, those two Closes of Land called by the name Little Clothers, lying in the Liberty of Willenhall, in the Parish of Wolverhampton, on condition that his said brother should pay or cause to be paid 30s. a year out of the rent of the said two Closes of land, as follows; that is to say, to the Minister of Willenhall 6s. 8d. a year to preach a sermon on New Year's Day; and unto Poor Housekeepers 8s. in bread yearly, upon New Year's Day, at the Chapel as the Chapelwardens should think fit; and to the Chapelwardens for their trouble 4d.; and 13s. yearly to one of the Chapelwardens and to the Overseer of the Poor to be given in bread to such Poor Housekeepers as they should think fit, and carry the said bread to, from house to house, upon the first day of July; and he directed that the Officers for trouble should have 12 pence apiece: And in the event of his brother's death without issue, he gave the Closes, paying the aforesaid 30s. yearly as above directed to the right heir of the Pedleys for ever.

The premises charged with this annuity of 30s. are at present the property of Mr. George Bailey, in right of his wife, to whom they descended as heir to her brother, Charles Pedley, the great-nephew of the testator.

The several payments of 6s. 8d. to the Minister and 8s. and 13s. for bread, appear to have been annually made; but the bread having been distributed by the Pedley family themselves, or persons deputed by them, without the intervention of the Chapelwarden or Overseer, the fees of 2s. 4d. to these Officers have been hitherto withheld, and are indeed unnoticed in a Will of James Pedley, dated in 1792, whereby he devises the Closes in question to the above-named Charles Pedley, describing them as subject to the other payments of 27s. 8d. only.

Mr. Bailey has, however, expressed his readiness to supply the omission in future, and to pay the bread money, or deliver the bread to the Officers of the Township to be distributed by them according to the directions of the donor.

The distributions appear to have been hitherto made respectively on New Year's Day and at Midsummer, among Poor Old Widows and other Poor of the Township.

3.—CHARITIES OF JOHN TOMKYS AND GEORGE WELCH.

At a Court Baron held for the Manor of Stowheath, on 29th May, 1781, the lords of the manor, at the request of certain persons being Chapelwardens, and certain others being Overseers of the Poor of the liberty of Willenhall, and of certain others, being three of the principal Inhabitants of Willenhall, on behalf of themselves and others, the inhabitants of Willenhall, by the hands of the Steward, according to the custom of the manor, gave, granted, and delivered to Joshua Fletcher, of Willenhall, and Catherina, his wife, all those three Closes or parcels of land, containing together five acres, or thereabouts, theretofore enclosed from the waste or common-land called Shepwell Green, within the liberty of Willenhall, for their natural lives and the life of the survivor, with remainder to the heirs and assigns of the said Joshua Fletcher for ever, subject to the payment of 20s. on St. Thomas's Day yearly for ever, to the Chapelwardens and Overseers of the Poor for the liberty of Willenhall, to be by them paid or applied to or for the use of the Poor of the said liberty of Willenhall, yearly and every year for ever on St. Thomas's Day aforesaid, at the Vestry of the said Chapel, according to their discretion, it being the interest of £20, £10 thereof being theretofore given by one

John Tomkys, and the other £10 theretofore given by one George Welch, to and for the use of the said Poor.

These premises are now the property of John Fletcher, by whom the annuity of 20s. is duly paid to the officers of the Township. This payment is distributed on New Year's Day among the Poor of the liberty in small sums not generally exceeding 6d. to each individual.

4.—JOHN BATES'S CHARITY.

This Charity consists of the sum of £5, which appears to have been left by John Bate some time before the year 1701; the interest to be yearly distributed among the Poor of Willenhall on St. Thomas's Day.

The principal was placed at interest on 21 December, 1701, in the hands of Joseph Hincks, on the security of his bond; and the interest appears to have been duly paid by himself and his heirs successively. It is now paid by Thomas Hincks on St. Thomas's Day annually to fifteen Poor Widows of the Township in shares of 4d. each.

The founders of the "lost" Prestwood Charity were doubtless members of the family mentioned in Chapter VII. as resident in Willenhall as early as 1409; Prestwood, be it noted, was also the name of an ancient moated farm and homestead in Wednesfield. The name of Prestwood is again mentioned, as are also the names of the other Willenhall benefactors, Bates and Tomkiss, in the endowment deeds of 1607, quoted in Chapter XXI. As to the Welch family, their homestead in Willenhall stood in the location known as Welch End.

Concerning Pedley's Charity, which has not been distributed these 50 years, the Churchwardens have, as recently as 1895, made earnest attempts at its recovery. The lands once chargeable for the dole were identified as Shares Acres, lying between the canal and the road leading to New Invention from Monmer Lane. The property, however, was found to be in the hands of the Trustees of the late W. E. Jones; and as, through the remissness of someone, the estate had been sold and conveyed without due provision for the payment of the annuity once charged upon it, the Trustees had not power to make such payment. While the minerals under this land have been yielding wealth, the Poor have been defrauded from their rightful share in the same.

Painstaking inquiries for the other "lost charities" have also been made, but with no success. For many years the Incumbent and Wardens have provided and distributed a Dole of 40 loaves, for which there has been no legal responsibility resting upon them.

In 1881 Jeremiah Hartill gave £200 to the Vicar and Wardens, which was invested in Consols, and the interest is annually distributed on January 1st amongst twenty poor people of the township. The Hartill Charity and the Tomkys and Welch Doles are the only ones now administered.

* * * * *

Thirty or more years ago a Mr. Stokes gave the Incumbent of Willenhall £500 to be applied in his absolute discretion for the benefit of St. Giles's School. The interest until recently was applied by him for that purpose. The principal has recently been spent in purchase of an extended playground for the new Infant Schools, and in the part purchase of a site for a new Mixed Department, adjacent thereto.

A few years after the passing of Sir Robert Peel's Act of 1847, advantage was taken of it to split the populous area of the ancient chapelry into new district parishes; and by 1855 the said chapelry was divided into three nearly equal parts, the new parishes of St. Stephen and Holy Trinity, leaving to St. Giles's Church Bentley and the remaining portion of the Willenhall township. The fourth daughter parish, St. Anne's, came a few years later.

St Stephen's Church, in Wolverhampton Street, was erected mainly through the exertions of its first vicar, the Rev. T. W. Fletcher, M.A., and opened in 1854, seven years after its ecclesiastical district had been formed. Mr. Fletcher died in 1890, and the living is now held by the Rev. Herbert Percy Stevens, M.A. This parish maintains a Parochial Hall and Mission at Portobello.

St. Anne's Church, Spring Bank, was built largely as a memorial to his wife by Mr. H. Jeavon. It was consecrated in 1861.

Holy Trinity Church (Short Heath) Vicarage and Schools were all built by the Rev. Dr. Rosedale, the first vicar of the parish, and father of the present vicar of St. Giles's. His labours commenced in a Mission Room at the Brown Jug Inn, Sandbeds, and he trained several very earnest men for the ministry, including the Rev. John Bailey, first vicar of the Pleck Church, Walsall, and the Rev. — Pritchard, vicar of Blakenall Church, Bloxwich. The jubilee of the building of the church was held about 1905. The Rev. — Wood was the second vicar, the Rev. G. W. Johnson the third, and the present vicar is the Rev. G. C. W. Pimbury.

A Mission Room at New Invention completes the list of Anglican Establishments in Willenhall.

In connection with St. Giles's a Men's and a Junior Men's Club have recently been established; and among other projects for further developments in the parochial machinery is a Mission Room at Shepwell Green. This movement was initiated some years ago when the Rev. H. Edwards was acting as Curate during the illness of the Rev. Mr. Fisher; a site has recently been purchased, in the anticipation that the Mission in due time will develop into a new ecclesiastical parish.

Dr. Hartill, as Churchwarden, was instrumental in securing a grant of £700 from a bequest of £15,000 left for Church objects by a Miss Green, with which to increase the endowment of Holy Trinity Church, Short Heath; this was supplemented by another £700 from the Ecclesiastical Commissioners; while in the following year a further sum of £700 from each source was also obtained for increasing the endowment of St. Anne's Church.

XXIII.—The Fabric of the Church.

As already discovered (Chapter VII.), a church has existed in Willenhall since the 13th century. It was at first a small chapel-of-ease, and seems to have been dedicated in pre-Reformation times to a non-biblical patron, Saint Giles.

The first edifice, as a mere chapel of accommodation, was in all probability a very primitive structure, constructed entirely of timber cut from the adjacent forest of Cannock. But when it became a chantry also, the original structure may have been replaced by a more elaborate edifice, in the style which is generally known as half-timbered.

Soon after the Reformation the mother church of Wolverhampton was pewed on a plan for the specifically allotted accommodation of all the parishioners, when the centre aisle was given to the inhabitants of Wolverhampton, the south aisle was set apart for the people of Bilston, and the north aisle was appropriated to Wednesfield and Willenhall. In those days, as previously explained, the law supposed that every adult person attended church on Sundays; there was, in fact, a penalty for absence enforcible by law.

With regard to Willenhall's timber-constructed church, there is evidence that in 1660 it was in a deplorable condition through fire ravages. After the Reformation it became a practice for collections to be made in the churches throughout the country to provide funds for the repair or rebuilding of parish churches which had fallen into a state of dilapidation beyond the means of its own parishioners to make good; or for other charitable purposes in which the needs of the one seemed to call for the help of the many. These collections were authorised to be made by Royal Letters Patent, through official documents known as Briefs; and entries of these are to be found in most Parish Registers till the middle of the 18th century, when their frequency through the complaisance of the Court of Chancery was considered such an abuse that it was ordered for the future that their issue should be granted only after a formal application to Quarter Sessions. Thus we find records in the Tipton Registers of no less than seven collections made there between 1657 and 1661 for the relief of distress through fire and other causes in Desford, Southwold, Drayton (Salop), Oxford, East Hogborne, Chichester, and Milton Abbey.

Willenhall called for this form of national assistance in 1660, as entries of a Brief on its behalf have been found as far apart as Chatham, in Kent, and Woodborough, in Notts, and may doubtless be traced in various parish registers up and down the country. Here is a copy of the Nottinghamshire entry:—

September ye 23, 1660.

COLLECTED at ye Parish Church and among ye Inhabitants of Woodbourogh for and towards the Reliefe of ye distressed inhabitants of Willenhall, in ye County of Stafford, being Commended hityr [hereto] by ye King's Majestyes Letters Patents with ye gorat Sale [Great Seal] for and towards their loss by fire, ye sum of 4s. 10d.

Witness,

JOHN ALLATT,

Minister.

JAMES JOB,
HENRY MOORELAW,

Churchwardens.

[It has been romantically suggested by a local writer that the "burning of Willenhall" was an act of revenge perpetrated by the Puritans of Lichfield and the vicinity for the succour given at Bentley Hall in 1651 to the fugitive Charles II.; and that these church collections are evidence of the personal interest taken by that monarch on his Restoration, in the place which had afforded him shelter in his hour of direst need. Two considerations will immediately dispel any such illusion. First, the Briefs were very commonplace affairs, as already shown; secondly, displays of Stuart gratitude were just as rare. All the reward commonplace affairs, as already shown; secondly, displays of Stuart gratitude were just as rare. All the reward Charles vouchsafed to the devoted Lanes was the cheap honour of an augmentation of the family arms, and the scanty gift of £1,000 to Jane Lane. Allusion has been made (Chapter XIII.) to the Royal fugitive taking advantage of the hiding-place afford by the "priest's hole" at Moseley Hall where Charles was loyally secreted by Jesuitic and other priestly adherents, though they might have pocketed a reward of £10,000 by betraying him—yet in after years this ungrateful prince had no compunction in signing more than twenty death warrants against Romanist priests, merely for the crime of being priests!]

To resume our history of Willenhall Church: What was manifestly a "restored" chapel was in 1727 consecrated by Edward, Lord Bishop of Coventry and Lichfield, on the same day that Bilston Chapel was consecrated; but the building could have been scarcely worth the attempt, as twenty years later it had to be entirely replaced.

On August 14th of the year 1727, the Bishop having first consecrated Bilston Chapel, in the presence of a large assembly of the local clergy, which included the Rev. R. Ames and two other prebendaries; the vicars of Walsall and Dudley; Mr. Tyrer, curate of Tettenhall; Mr. Gibbons, minister of Codsall; Mr. Varden, rector of Darlaston; Mr. Perry, curate of Wednesbury; and Mr. Holbrooke, curate of Willenhall; his lordship proceeded to Willenhall in a coach and four, where the ceremony of Consecration "in Latine" was repeated upon what was merely a renovated building. After which Squire Lane, of Bentley, gave a splendid entertainment in celebration of the event.

A "chappel-yard for the Burial of the Dead," which had been added, was consecrated at the same time, and, strangely enough—as if the parishioners of Willenhall were eager to signalise their acquisition of such a parochial institution as a graveyard—the first interment was made the selfsame day.

About the middle of the eighteenth century there was a wave of zeal for church extension, on which we find Wolverhampton carried along rather freely; for within the short space of ten years, under the auspices of Dr. Pennistan Booth, the enterprising Dean, the building of four chapels-of-ease was projected. These daughter churches were:—

1746—Wednesfield (Advowson of which was vested in Walter Gough and his heirs).

1748—Willenhall.

1753—Bilston.

1755—St. John's (the new building was injured by fire, and not consecrated till 1760).

From the Registers is gleaned the following issue of a writ to release sequestration of fees:—

> Memorandum. March 4, 1748.—The Faculty for Rebuilding and enlarging ye Chapel of Willenhall authorized ye then present Ministr, ye Revd. Titus Neve to charge and receive for Breaking up ye Ground or Building a Vault in ye said Chapel ye sum of two Guineas and also one Guinea for opening ye same at any time afterwards to him and his successors. The Intention of this Siquise was to prevent frequent interments which are a common annoyance to ye Living Votaries for whose use ye Chapel was erected.

From the Diary of Dr. Richard Wilkes is extracted the following illuminative entry—a contemporary record of the state of the ancient edifice:—

> May 6, 1748.—This day I set out the foundation of a new church in this town; for the old one being half timber, the sills, pillars, etc., were so decayed that the inhabitants, when they met together, were in great danger of being killed. It appeared to me, that the old church must have been rebuilt, at least the middle aisle of it; and that the first fabrick was greatly ornamented, and must have been the gift of some rich man, or a number of such, the village then being but thin of inhabitants, and, before the iron manufacture was begun here, they could not have been able to erect such a fabrick; but no date, or hint relating to it, was to be found; nor is anything about it come to us by tradition.

Willenhall's rebuilt church was completed in 1749, and had a formal re-opening on October 30th of that year. An entry in the Registers (which has already been quoted in Chapter XVIII.) seems to intimate that the regular services were not resumed till January 20th, 1750.

This edifice was a fair specimen of the crudities which went to make up the "churchwarden architecture" of the period; consisting mainly of a plain, box-like nave, pierced on either side by half a dozen staring oblong windows, and having in the whole of its hulk not one curved line or rounded form by which relief could be afforded to the eye at any single point. At one end of this unimposing structure was a flattened scutiform excrescence which served as the chancel; from the others rose the tower, the only feature by which the building could be recognised as a church. The tower, not to put the rest of the church out of countenance, was equally crude; its window piercings being as debased in the Gothic style as was its cornice in quasi-classical; and topped as it was by a low-pitched hipped roof or squat pyramid, from the point of which rose high into the air the famous Willenhall weathercock—the brazen bird flaunting itself aloft, as if deriving its defiance from the aggressive-looking furcated finials which surrounded it at the four angles.

This church endured only for about a century, being replaced in 1867 by the present edifice, erected at a cost of £7,000, raised by public subscription. The Chairman of the Committee for the rebuilding was Mr. R. D. Gough, who, with his wife, contributed £1,700. Other large contributors were Mrs. Stokes (with £505), and the Vicar and Trustees (who gave £1,000).

St. Giles's Church is now a substantial stone building in the Decorated style, consisting of nave, aisles, chancel and transepts, and having at the west end a lofty square tower, terminated with a pinnacle at each angle. The new fane was soon adorned by the insertion of a number of stained glass windows; the large east window was presented by Mr. R. D. Gough; others were given by the Lords of the Manor of Stow Heath (emblazoning the arms of Leveson-Gower and Giffard); by the Earl of Lichfield and the Rev. Charles Lane (also heraldically distinguished); one was put in as a memorial to members of the Clemson family; and another to commemorate Mrs. Anwell, a connection of the Gough family.

The work of enlarging the church was undertaken in 1897 in memory of the late Incumbent, Mr. Fisher; and a fine organ was installed in celebration of Queen Victoria's Diamond Jubilee. Also at the same time choir stalls were introduced, the choristers being brought from the gallery, which latter feature was rightly removed altogether. Among the improvements promoted by the Incumbent and his energetic churchwardens, Dr. John T. Hartill and Mr. H. H. Walker, of Bentley Hall, were the enlargement of the churchyard and the scheme for providing a church house.

As the new incumbent, Mr. Rosedale, was a nephew of Mrs. Gough, the generous contributor to the rebuilding fund of 1865–7, just mentioned, it was suggested that the house she occupied might fittingly be transformed to serve as a Parsonage.

* * * * *

Almost from the time pews were first put into churches, seats became appurtenant to certain family mansions, and by custom descended from ancestor to heir, without any ecclesiastical concurrence. Instances of such proprietary pews having been bequeathed by will have occurred in Willenhall within comparatively recent times. Here is an extract from the will of Thomas Hartill, dated June 5th, 1777:—

> I give and bequeath to my Son, Abraham Hartill, the fourth part of a seat in the Chapel, No. 4 in B row an all so one 4 part of a seat in F row near the Dore. . . . and I bequeath to my Daughter, Phœbe Read, one Fourth part of a seate No. 4 in B row and also one Fourth part of a seate in the Chapel in F row near the Dore.

Similar testamentary disposals appear in the will of Isaac Hartill, dated 27 May, 1818:—

> I give and devise to my Son, Isaac Hartill, all that my moiety or half part of the seat or pew, being No. 10 in the South Aisle within the Church or Chapel of Willenhall aforesaid, to hold to him my said son, Isaac, his heirs and assigns tor ever. . . .
>
> I give and devise unto my said Son, Ephraim Hartill, one moiety or equal half part of, and in my seat, or pew, being number 4 in the South Aisle within the Church or Chapel aforesaid, to hold to my said Son, Ephraim, his Heirs, and assigns for ever. And I also give and devise unto my daughter, Mary Atkins, the other moiety or equal half part or share of the said last mentioned seat or pew, to hold to my said Daughter Mary Atkins, her heirs and assigns for ever.

Of like purport is the following extract from codicil to the will of Samuel Hartill, dated June 9, 1821; probate Nov. 12, 1821:—

> I give devise and bequeath to my nephew Henry Bratt, all that my seat or pew or part or share thereof being number eleven in A in Willenhall Church, to hold to him his heirs, executors administrators or assigns according to the tenure of the said property. I give devise and bequeath to my Brother-in-law, Isaac Hartill in my Will named all my other Seats or Pews or parts or shares of seats or pews in Willenhall Church aforesaid to hold to him his heirs executors administrators or assigns according to the tenure of the said property.

Thus much in witness of the heritable nature of Church Pews; now for documentary evidences of the trafficking in such properties (all relating to Willenhall Church):—

> 19, Jan., 1750. Recd. of Tho. Harthil, John Parker and Joseph Wood three pound one and sixpence for the seat

behind ye Dore in F, sixteen shillings and sixpence being allow'd them for 6s. 8d. of ground by

RICHD. WILKES.

A 12.

6 Jan, 1750.—Recd. of Jos. Clemson, Jos. Chandler. Jo'n Buttler, Jo'n Turner, Jno. Smith, Stephen Perry, the Sum of two Ginnies for Wainscots and for 2ft. 3in. of Ground five and sevenpence halfpenny by

RICHD. WILKES.

£2 7s. 7½d.

"I hereby acknowledge that I have this day had and received from Abraham Hartill . . . the sum of One Pound Fifteen Shillings for the full and absolute purchase sale value and Consideration of all those my sittings kneelings Parts or shares of and in two different seats or pews and standing and being on the left-hand side in the first Ile and numbered with the figures 11 and 12 in the Church or Chapel of Willenhall aforesaid, and which said sittings kneelings Parts or shares of the said seats or pews I do hereby Warrant unto the said Abraham Hartill his Heirs Exors Admors and Assigns against me, my Heirs Exors Admors and Assigns and that I my Heirs Exors, Admors or Assigns shall and will at any time or times hereafter upon the request and Costs of the said Abraham Hartill His Heirs &c. . . . execute any further or other Conveyances and Assurance of the said sittings, &c. . . . unto and to the use of the said Abraham Hartill . . . free from all manner of Incumbrances whatsoever and the said Abraham Hartill Doth hereby agree for Francis Chandler and Ann his wife to use and enjoy that part or share of the above seat or pew numbered 11 for and during the term of their Natural lives and for the longest survivor of them without expence, but for no other privilege to be allowed to any other person Whatsoever. In Witness whereof the said Francis Chandler the seller of the above sittings kneelings parts or shares of the seats or pews above mentioned hath set his hand this nineteenth day of February 1790.

Witness

FRANCIS CHANDLER.

Wm. Perkin.
Saml Hartill."

"Received January 24 1783 of Isaac Hartill The Sum of Two Pounds in full for Halfe a Seat Number 10 in E In Willenhall Chappell

By mee The Mark X of RICHD. HARTILL.
Witness Jonah Hartill."

"Willenhall April 26th 1791 Received then of Abrm Hartill Thirteen Shillings For my Whole Right in a seat in the Chapel No. 12 in A Row.

STEPHEN PERREY.

Willenhall April 26th 1791 Received then of."

Of this last voucher there is a duplicate copy bearing a twopenny receipt stamp.

XXIV.—Dissent, Nonconformity, and Philanthrophy.

Inasmuch as Bentley Hall lies within the confines of Willenhall, this place must always be associated with the rise and early history of Wesleyanism. The episode of John Wesley being haled by the Wednesbury rioters before Justice Lane at Bentley Hall (1743) belongs to the general history of the denomination, and there is no need to repeat the story here.

The reader may be referred to "The History of Methodism in the Wednesbury Circuit," by the Rev. W. J. Wilkinson, published by J. M. Price, Darlaston, 1895; and for ampler detail to "Religious Wednesbury," by the present writer, 1900.

That the evangelical missioning of John Wesley was peculiarly suited to the religious and social needs of the eighteenth century, and nowhere more so than among the proletariat of the mining and manufacturing Midlands, is now a generally accepted truism. There is no direct evidence that the great evangelist himself ever preached in Willenhall, but the appearance on the scene of some of the earliest Methodist preachers may be taken for granted. For were not the prevailing sins of cockfighting and bull-baiting, and all the other popular brutalities of the period, to be combated in Willenhall as much as in Darlaston or Wednesbury? And where the harvest was, were not the reapers always forthcoming?

According to Mr. A. Camden Pratt, in his "Black Country Methodism," the earliest Methodist services were open-air meetings held round a big boulder at the corner of Monmore Lane. Then the nucleus of a Willenhall congregation was formed at a cottage in Ten House Row; outgrowing its accommodation here, a removal was next made to a farmhouse with a commodious kitchen at Hill End.

The leaders and preachers came from Darlaston, and it was not till 1830 that Willenhall was favoured with a resident "travelling preacher," and the provision of a Wesleyan Chapel—it was on the site of the present Wesleyan Day Schools. The cause flourished and grew mightily; chapels were established at Short Heath and Portobello, on the Walsall Road (1865), and on Spring Bank.

Mr. Pratt pays a high tribute to the efforts of the Tildesleys and the Harpers, but with a sense of justice he does not forget the mead of gratitude always due to those early pioneers from Darlaston, placing on the same bright scroll of fame the names of Foster, Wilkes, Rubery, Silcock, Bowen, and Banks.

In the earlier history of local Wesleyanism, one of its chief supporters was James Carpenter, founder of the existing firm of Carpenter and Tildesley. Another pillar of Wesleyanism was Jonah Tildesley, followed later in the good work by his two sons, Josiah and Jesse, his grandson Thomas, George Ley Pearce, and Isaac Pedley; and in a lesser degree by James Tildesley (who married Harriet Carpenter), and the late John Harper, founder of the Albion Works, now the largest place of employment in the town.

One outcome of the Wesleyan spirit was seen about the year 1820, when James Carpenter, George Pearce, William Whitehouse, and other leading inhabitants made a determined effort to put down some of the coarser sports by which the annual Wake was celebrated. Through their instrumentality many of the ringleaders in the brutal sports were summoned and brought to justice. The reformers dared to go even further—they lodged a complaint with the bishop of the diocese against "Parson Moreton" for encouraging these barbarous pastimes among the people. The bishop, however, professed that he was powerless to deal with the delinquent, owing to the exceptional manner in which he was appointed to the living. But the parson on his part was very wroth, and from his pulpit he solemnly forbade any one of the name of Carpenter, Pearce, or Whitehouse ever to enter the portals of Willenhall Church.

It cannot be said the injunction was enforced; but it is a fact that from that time many church-goers were driven into the Methodist fold.

The romantic side of the evangelisation of the Black Country has been idealised by Mr. J. C. Tildesley in his "Sketches of Early Methodism," a series of short stories founded on fact, and giving most graphic pictures of the moral and social condition of the neighbourhood at that time. This little volume may be regarded almost as one of the classics of the Wesleyan Book Room.

A short history of local Methodism, it may be mentioned, was deposited in the memorial stones of Wednesfield Chapel in 1885.

The existing Wesleyan Chapels, now under the direction of the Rev. A. Hann and the Rev. Walter Fytche, are five in number, namely, Union Street, Walsall Road, Monmer Lane, Short Heath, and High Street, Portobello. Though the denomination may be as strong as ever numerically, it can scarcely hope to rival its old-time membership in verve and vigour. In England fighting days never fail to produce fighting men.

Primitive Methodism first established itself at Monmer Lane, and then removed to Little London, but did not meet with much success at the outset, though it has now four flourishing chapels in the township. They are all at present under the direction of the Rev. C. L. Tack, and situated respectively at New Invention, Spring Bank, Lane Head, and Russell Street.

Nonconformity was first brought into Willenhall from Coseley, the brethren of the famous Darkhouse Chapel establishing a colony at Little London, where eventually they erected a pioneer Baptist Chapel. Of this chapel the Rev. A. Tettmar is now in charge; a second chapel in Upper Lichfield Street, at which the Rev. D. L. Lawrence ministers, and a third Baptist Chapel in New Road testify to the growth of the denomination in Willenhall. At one time the Baptists had day schools in the town.

The Roman Catholics first made their appearance in modern Willenhall some sixty years ago, when they established a small mission at the bottom of Union Street, afterwards building their resent chapel, which is dedicated to St. Mary, and of which the Rev. Walter Poulton (in succession to the Rev. W. P. Wells) is priest.

A mission of the Catholic Apostolic Brethren, served from Wolverhampton, completes the list of religious agencies now at work in Willenhall.

In the religious and social history of the place mention cannot be omitted of some few names which have earned the respect of the townspeople. Among them, James Tildesley, a large employer of labour, whose amiability, and kindness of heart exemplified that patriarchal relationship which once existed between master and men, anterior to the days of modern limited liability companies; George Ley Pearce, a Wesleyan of marked personality, and an eminently good man, whose memorial in the old Cemetery is thus inscribed:—

> ERECTED
> by voluntary subscription in memory of
> GEORGE LEY PEARCE
> (of Willenhall),
> who died December 31st, 1873,
> Aged 78;
> And was buried in the adjacent vault.

> For fifty years he zealously devoted himself to the work of visiting the sick and afflicted of this town, whether rich or poor, and was made a great blessing to many.
>
> His work was the outward expression of that Christ-like charity which pervaded his soul.

The opportunity to do good to our fellowmen comes to all, irrespective of sect or sex. One to embrace it with goodwill was Edith Florence Hartill, daughter of William Henry Hartill, who worked long and steadfastly in connection with the Bible Reading Union, never relaxing her efforts for the uplifting of the very poorest and most helpless of the community.

In the Market Place stands a public clock mounted upon a stone pedestal, having a watering-trough for cattle at its base. This was erected, as an inscription upon it testifies, as a memorial to the late Joseph Tonks, surgeon, "whose generous and unsparing devotion in the cause of alleviating human suffering" was "deemed worthy of public record." The memorialised, Mr. Joseph Tonks, M.R.C.S.E., L.A.H., was a native of the town, being a son of Mr. Silas Tonks, of the Forge Inn, Spring Bank. He began to practise in Willenhall about 1879, and soon made himself extremely popular among the working classes, and particularly with the Friendly Societies, who initiated the movement to provide this public memorial.

Without sorting into sects and creeds, let it be acknowledged that Willenhall has been fortunate in the number of its townsmen whose lives have been usefully and commendably spent in the public service and for the public good. Among those whose influence on the social and moral well-being of the place has not been without appreciable benefit, may be named Joseph Carpenter Tildesley, R. D. Gough, Josiah Tildesley, Clement Tildesley, Jesse Tildesley, Isaac Pedley, Henry Hall, Thomas Kidson, Henry Vaughan, W. E. Parkes, and J. H. James. Other appreciations will occur in our concluding chapters, as the names more fittingly happen under the topics yet to be dealt with.

Having brought to a conclusion Willenhall's ecclesiastical and religious history—and the largeness with which the church bulked on the lives of the people in past times must be held accountable for the lengthiness of this portion—we may now turn to the further consideration of its civil, social, and industrial history.

XXV.—Manorial Government.

Willenhall is a township of some 1,980 acres in extent, carved out of the ancient parish of Wolverhampton, and situated midway between that town and the town of Walsall, being about three miles distant from either. Strangely enough, Willenhall is included in the Hundred of Offlow, although Wolverhampton, of which it once formed a part, is in Seisdon Hundred. Willenhall has never been a civil parish (as previously explained), nor has it been a market town; the small open market held in its streets each week-end having grown up by prescription, but never legally established by grant of charter.

The place grew up as a hamlet on the banks of a little stream, just on the verge of Cannock Forest. As a village community it seems to have been subject, so soon as its outer limits had been defined, to three territorial lords. Reference to Chapter VI. will disclose that at Domesday (1086) three hides of land in Willenhall belonged to the king, and were part of the royal manor of Stowheath; two hides were the property of the Church of Wolverhampton, and constituted the prebendal manor of Willenhall; and a century or two later, the manor of Bentley, evidently carved out of the royal forest of Cannock, became included within this township.

Of STOWHEATH MANOR, the portions lying within Willenhall are a small part of the modern township, together with Short Heath, New Invention, Lanehead, Sandbeds, Little London, and Portobello. The remainder of this manor stretches beyond the Willenhall boundary into Bilston and Wolverhampton.

To a manor or lordship was usually attached a Court Baron, or domestic court of the lord, for the settling of disputes relating to property among the tenants, and for redressing misdemeanours and nuisances arising within the manor. The business was transacted by a jury or homage elected by and from the tenants.

How far the customary officers were chosen every year by the Willenhall Court Baron cannot now be ascertained. Doubtless appointments were made from time to time of such manorial tears as Hedgers and Ditchers, to look after the highways and byways, a Common Pinner to impound stray cattle, and Head boroughs or Petty Constables "to apprehend all vagrom men" whose room was esteemed more highly than their company.

The present lords of the Manor of Stowheath are the Duke of Sutherland, and W. T. C. Giffard, Esq., of Chillington; the Steward of the Manor is Mr. W. E. Stamer, of Lilleshall; and the Deputy-Steward Mr. Frederick T. Langley, of Wolverhampton. The Court Bailiff is Mr. H. G. Duncalfe, of

Wolverhampton, but none of the ancient customary officers are now elected; and as most of the copyholds have been enfranchised, no Court Baron for Stowheath has been held in Willenhall since 22nd December, 1865; till then it had taken place annually for many years at the house of Mr. George Baker, the Neptune Inn. Subsequently this manorial court was held at the Bank, Cock Street, Wolverhampton, and now more privately at the offices of the Deputy-Steward, in that town, which was anciently within the jurisdiction of two manors, Stowheath and Wolverhampton.

THE MANOR OF WILLENHALL, which, though prebendal, is impropriate, comprises the rest of the township; of this manor the Baron Barnard is the present lord, and the sole recipient of all tithes from Willenhall, Short Heath, and Wednesfield.

A glimpse of the mediæval village of Willenhall was obtained in Chapters VIII. and XI.; it is clear the prebendal manor remained always a taxable area for the mere production of tithes, and it was the royal manor of Stowheath, when it had passed into the hands of a subject, which developed into the community in the midst of which the "mansum capitale," or manor house, was erected.

By whom or when a manor house was first set up in Willenhall is not known; but it is not improbable that the lordship of Stowheath, soon after it passed out of the hands of the King, was acquired by a Leveson, who seated himself on the estate, reserving to himself the portion which lay nearest his mansion (demesne lands), and distributing the rest among his tenants (tenemental lands).

The house in which the Levesons resided, as previously recorded, was situated on the east side of Stafford Street; the Midland Railway now runs through the site, but before the line was cut, and whilst the mines remained ungotten, traces of its ancient moat were clearly discernible.

The residence now known as the Manor House, and occupied by Dr J. T. Hartill, though it has no connection with the manorial mansion of the Leveson family, is not without some association with the manorial form of government. It appears that upwards of half a century ago, when the late Jeremiah Hartill (uncle of the present occupant of the house) was taking his full share in the public life of Willenhall, it was most difficult, if not next to impossible, to get copyhold land in this manor enfranchised.

At that time there was a very considerable amount of property in Willenhall held by this old-world tenure, and this induced Mr. Jeremiah Hartill to take a very prominent part in the local efforts which were then being made to introduce the principle of compulsory enfranchisement. As the result of a national movement in this direction an Act was passed in 1841 to provide a statutory method of enfranchisement; and the matter was carried still further in 1852 by another Act, which introduced the principle of compulsory enfranchisement.

Mr. Hartill had at that time recently built himself a new house (1847), when, as the local leader in a movement which had been brought so far on the road to success, he was invited to a public dinner in recognition of his public-spirited efforts. One of the speakers at the banquet, in proposing the health of the guest of the evening, suggested that as Mr. Jeremiah Hartill had fought so successfully in helping to overcome the opposition of the Lords of the Manor to this measure of land reform, his new house might not inappropriately be dubbed the Manor House. The suggestion was heartily (no pun intended) approved by all present, and by that name the house has ever since been known.

The names of the chief residents in Willenhall in 1327 may be gleaned from the Subsidy Roll given in Chapter IX.; very similar names occur in another list of the taxpayers to the Scotch War of 1333. Some few held land under certain specified rents and free services, and from these came the earliest freeholders; many more held by the baser tenure of the lord's will, and having nothing to show except the copy of the rolls made by the Steward of the Lord's Court, were known as copyholders.

The vast importance of these Court Rolls may be gathered from Chapter XXI. The Court Rolls of the Manor of Stowheath now in existence commence on 4 January, 1645; but in the chapter referred to mention of a "Leete" being held in Wolverhampton much earlier will be found.

The residue of the Manor being uncultivated, was termed the lord's waste, and served for public roads, and for common or pasture to both the lord and his tenants. Reference to the enclosure of the last remnants of the "waste" was quoted in the Report of 1825 on the Tomkys and Welch Charities (Chapter XXII.).

There were two kinds of enclosures, however, all made in the last few centuries; the enclosure of the open commons or wastes, and the enclosure of the common fields. "Willenhall Field," mentioned in the "Report on Prestwood's Dole," as lying along the highway towards Darlaston, was arable land, not pasture. For anciently there was a common field system in every parish, and "Willenhall Field" was the area cultivated co-operatively by the whole of the parishioners or group of individuals.

In 1377 the MANOR OF BENTLEY was held "in capite," that is, direct from the King, by one who called himself after his estate, William de Bentley. He held it for rendering to Edward III. the feudal service of "Keeping" the King's Hay of Bentley within the royal Forest of Cannock—the Forest was then divided into a number of "hays" or bailiwicks. (See "Chronicles of Cannock Chase," p. 14.)

The estate seems to have descended to him from his grandfather, to whom it had been granted in the reign of Edward II.; and it is noteworthy that his wife, Alianora, was a Leveson.

In 1421 William Griffiths established his right to Bentley, and in 1430 it was conveyed to Richard Lone de la Hide. Of the family of this Richard Lone of the Hyde there were afterwards two branches; one, the Hamptons, of Stourton Castle, and the other, the Lanes, of Bentley.

The halo of romance which grew up around Bentley Hall during the seigniory of the Lanes is well known. It was the scene of Charles II.'s wonderful escape from the Roundheads, under the protection of Jane Lane, whom he was afterwards wont to call his "Guardian Angel"; it was the critical scene of John Wesley's adventure in the hands of the Wednesbury mob. The mansion has since been rebuilt.

The Lanes sold the Manor of Bentley in 1748 to Joseph Turton, of Wolverhampton, and he in turn sold it to the first Lord Anson, ancestor of the present holder.

The Manor comprises 1,200 acres, none of which is now copyhold. There was formerly a Court Leet jurisdiction, but everything connected with ancient manorial government has disappeared. The Earl of Lichfield is sole owner, except for a few acres belonging to the church, and the portions which have been acquired by the local authority for the Cemetery and the Sewerage Works.

Bentley is a parish without a church, or a chapel, and until the Willenhall District Council recently made a Cemetery there, it was also without a burial ground.

Bentley has but a scant population, and contains not a single inn. Its living history seems to have centred almost entirely round the old family mansion of the Lanes.

In 1660 a tax was levied on the fire-hearth of every dwelling-house, and the amount collected under this grievous impost in Willenhall was returned as £9 14s. 3d., representing 97 hearths. These figures seem to indicate that in the reign of Charles II. the population of the place, including the large hall at Bentley, could not have exceeded 500.

XXVI.—Modern Self-Government.

For centuries the Manorial and the Parochial forms of government ran together side by side in this country, till these two antiquated ideas of feudal lordship and church temporalities had to give way before the growing democratic principle of elective representation, and they were eventually supplanted by the modern methods of popular self-government.

In the reign of Elizabeth—say, half a century after the suppression of the monasteries which had hitherto succoured the poor—we get the first of our Poor Laws, accompanied by the rise of the Overseer, and by much added importance to the office of Churchwarden, or, as he was called in Willenhall, the Chapel-warden. The establishment of Church doles goes a long way to explain how strenuously the community strove to evade its liability to the poor, and it is probable that Willenhall did not establish its small workhouse till the eighteenth century. This was superseded when the Wolverhampton Union was constituted in 1834.

In 1776 the sum of £294 14s. 3d. had to be collected for poor rates in Willenhall, a sum which by 1785 had grown to £548 14s. 2d., and which for some years later averaged upwards of £500.

The Vestry, or public assembly of parishioners, would supplement these feeble efforts at local government by choosing not only Chapelwardens, but Parish Constables and the Waywardens. The custody of the stocks was entrusted to the former, while the latter were supposed to superintend the amateur efforts of the parishioners to repair their own highways, every one being then liable to furnish either manual labour or team work for this laudable public purpose.

Publicly elected and unsalaried Waywardens were naturally but feeble instruments to work with; so in the early nineteenth century, when coaching was at its zenith, this antiquated and ineffective system was superseded in Willenhall, as in many other places, by an elected Highway Board, charged with the duty of looking after all highways and common streets, ancient bridges, ditches, and watercourses. In a dilettante sort of way this Board was also a sanitary body.

In 1734 Willenhall is recorded to have suffered from a plague called the "Bloody flux," which carried away its victims in a very few hours after the seizure. It is stated in the Parish Registers that there were buried in this year 82 persons, which was 67 in excess of the previous year. The population then was under 1,000.

Cholera and other epidemic scourges having made it apparent that beyond preserving the peace and mending the roads, the paramount duty of local self-government was to protect the people's health, Willenhall in 1854 showed itself alive to this fact by adopting the new Public Health Acts and calling into being its first Local Board.

Nothing can convey an idea of the material blessings which resulted from this better than a glance at the vital statistics relating to Willenhall. The death-rate per thousand—

From 1845 to 1851 was	29
,, 1851 ,, 1860 ,,	26.8
,, 1861 ,, 1870 ,,	23.8
,, 1891 ,, 1900 ,,	20.2
,, 1901 ,, 1906 ,,	16.9

It was not till 1866, however, that the Board appointed its first medical officer of health, Dr. Parke. He was shortly afterwards succeeded by Mr. William Henry Hartill, and upon his death, in 1888, the present medical officer of heath, Dr. J. T. Hartill, was appointed. The chief executive officers in succession have been Mr. E. Wilcox (who was not a solicitor), Mr. John Clark, and the present clerk, Mr. Rowland Tildesley, appointed in 1894.

In the meantime the population, particularly in the newer outlying districts, had been growing rapidly. The population of Willenhall at the first national census in 1801 was only 3,143, and the growth in the early decades was slow, as these figures disclose:

In 1811 the population was	3,523
,, 1821	3,965
,, 1831	5,834
,, 1841	8,695
,, 1851	11,933
,, 1861	17,256

With the growth thus becoming so rapid, it was thought desirable, in 1872, to erect Short Heath into a separate Sanitary Authority. The area allotted to the Short Heath Board of Health was that north of the Birmingham Canal, but the village of Short Heath itself remained part of the Township of Willenhall.

The census returns for Willenhall, minus Short Heath, have

1871 it had a population of	15,903
1881	16,067
1891	16,851
1901	18,515

After the passing of Sir H. H. Fowler's Local Government Act in 1895, both authorities became Urban District Councils. Short Heath then as a separate township had its area extended to take in Short Heath village, with New Invention, Lanehead, Sandbeds, Lucknow, Fibbersley, in addition to the former Local Board district, together with a slice from the old Wednesfield Local Board district added on its Essington side.

No part of what used to be called Stow Heath was in Willenhall Township, the extreme western boundary of the latter being Stow Heath Lane.

Modern Willenhall, although without public parks or pleasure grounds, and not yet possessing public baths, is fairly well equipped for its size and rateable value. It has its Public Offices, but no Town Hall; it has a Free Library, established in 1875, and a full complement of efficient primary schools. In 1877 it established its own School Board under the Act of 1870, but under the later Act of 1902 its educational affairs became vested in the Staffordshire County Council.

Willenhall had its own Waterworks at Monmore Lane as early as 1852; it now takes its supply from the Wolverhampton Corporation, who purchased the old works in 1868. Its old Gas Works in Lower Lichfield Street have been taken over by Short Heath; and Willenhall is now supplied by the Willenhall Gas Company, the present system of public street lighting being that of the very efficient incandescent burner.

The Sewerage of the town was completed in 1890. There are two public cemeteries; the Old Cemetery provided about 1851 under the Burial Acts, and the newer one at Bentley, established under the Act of 1879.

The Police are, as in most townships, under the control of the Staffordshire County Council; and Petty Sessions are held once a week (on Mondays). Seventy years ago Willenhall had a Court of Requests for the recovery of debts up to £5.

For Parliamentary representation Willenhall formed a portion of Staffordshire till the great Reform Bill of 1832 made Wolverhampton a borough, when it became part of that more important urban constituency.

For communication with the outer world Willenhall has had the advantage of the London and North-Western Railway from the earliest possible time—

since the "Grand Junction Railway" (commenced in 1835) was opened to public traffic on July 4th, 1837. Great were the rejoicings, and prodigious the wonderment when the first train passed through on that memorable day. Since the later decades of the last century the Midland Railway has also tapped Willenhall.

The town is equally well supplied with tramways; the Wolverhampton District Electric Tramways, Limited, controlling three lines, to Wolverhampton, to Bilston, and Darlaston respectively; while the Walsall Corporation afford facilities for communication with their thriving and go-ahead borough. It is worthy of note that the old-fashioned carrier's cart is not obsolete in Willenhall; this is probably because its staple industries provide so many small parcels for transmission to Wolverhampton, Birmingham, and other centres not too far distant.

The Wyrley and Essington Canal for heavy traffic was made in 1792, and is still a useful highway, particularly to the Cannock Chase Collieries.

XXVII.—The Town of Locks and Keys.

Willenhall is "the town of locks and keys"; its staple industry has been described in such graceful and felicitous terms by Elihu Burritt (see his "Walks in the Black Country," pp. 206–214, written in 1868) that the present writer at once confesses the inadequacy of his poor pen to say anything new on the subject, engaging as it is.

The great American writer, be it noted, does not fail at the very outset to pay a well-deserved tribute to James Carpenter Tildesley, as the foremost authority on the subject, and compliments him on the versatility displayed in his article on Locks and Keys, contributed to that co-operative literary work, "Birmingham and the Midland Hardware District," which was specially issued for the British Association meeting at Birmingham in 1865.

The lockmakers of antiquity worked in wood and not in metal, a key consisting of hard wood pegs being made to turn in a wooden lock of loose pegs. The Romans first introduced the iron key with wards instead of pegs.

The subject is full of interest; for lock-making is among the most ancient of the mechanical crafts, and has for centuries afforded a wide and ample scope as one of the branches of industrial art. As in many other industrial crafts the religious enthusiasm of the Middle Ages impelled the artist-mechanic to throw his whole soul into the manipulation and adornment of his keys, key-hole escutcheons, and other parts of door-fastening furniture. With his steel pencil and gravers, his chisels and his drills, the craftsman of olden times produced an article of utility which was at the same time a work of art. Will the Art Classes of modern Willenhall be able to achieve as much for the staple industry of the town as did the whole-souled enthusiasm of the Middle Ages?

The Gothic key, usually of iron or of bronze, was generally plain; but after the Renaissance the best efforts of the locksmiths' art were directed to the decoration of the bow and the shaft, and many finely wrought specimens of ornamental old keys are still in existence.

On the utilitarian side of our subject, industrial history records that we are indebted to the Chinese for unpickable locks of the lever and tumbler principle; and to the Dutch for the combination or letter-lock. The latter ingenious contrivance contained four revolving rings, on which were engraved the letters of the alphabet, and they had to be turned in such a way as to spell some pre-arranged word of four letters, as O P E N, or A M E N, before the lock could be opened.

Allusion to this complex contrivance is made by the poet Carew in some verses written in the year 1620—

> As doth a lock
> That goes with letters—for till every one be known
> The lock's as fast as if you had found none.

Mechanical ingenuity in lock making has also expanded itself along the line of marvellous miniatures, in the production of toy locks so small that they could be worn as pendants or personal ornaments. Allusion will presently be made to a Willenhall specimen.

Another ingenious variety of locks was contrived to grab and hold the fingers of pilferers.

The first patent granted in England for a lock was in 1774; ten years later Joseph Bramah, of London, "the Napoleon of locks," patented his famous production, with which he challenged the whole world. The reward of 200 guineas which he offered to anyone who could pick his lock remained unclaimed for many years, till in the Exhibition year 1851 an American visitor named Hobbs took up the challenge, and succeeded, after a few days of persevering experiment, in overcoming the inviolability of it.

The sensation caused by this achievement was almost of national dimensions; but of more importance was the decided impetus it have to the inventive skill of lock makers, by demonstrating that Bramah had not yet arrived at finality in lock making; a great number of further improvements were soon forthcoming in the manufacture of these goods.

Chubb's patent was granted in 1818; this inventor declared it was possible to have the locks on the doors of every house in London opened by a different key, and yet have a master-key that would pass the whole of them. Chubb's world-famous concern is now located at Wolverhampton.

Dr. Plot, writing of this county in 1686, makes no mention of the trade being carried on in Willenhall, but gives some account of it in Wolverhampton; gossiping pleasantly on "sutes" of six or more locks, passable by one master-key, being sold round the country by the chapmen of his time; of the finely wrought keys he had seen; of the curious tell-tale locks which recorded the times they had been opened; and of one valuable Wolverhampton specimen containing chimes which could be set to "go" at any particular hour.

A local writer has said—on what authority is not stated—that Queen Elizabeth granted to the township of Willenhall the privilege of making all the locks required for State purposes; and argues from that profitable piece of State patronage the rapid growth of Willenhall, as evidenced by the fact that in 1660 when the Hearth Tax came to be levied this place paid on 13 more hearths than the mother town of Wolverhampton.

Dr. Wilkes has recorded that in his time Willenhall consisted of one long street, newly paved; and he then proceeds to say:—

> "The village did not begin to flourish till the iron manufactory was brought into these parts in the reign of Queen Elizabeth."

This may, or may not, refer to the making of locks and keys, but it certainly refers to the great devastation of Cannock Forest in providing charcoal for iron-smelting. The doctor continues:—

> "Since that time this place is become very populous, and more locks of all kinds are made here than in any other town of the same size in England or Europe. The better sort of which tradesmen have erected many good houses."

Some of these "good houses" are still standing; and as to the "populousness" of the place, there may have been 2,000 inhabitants at that time. A return has been given forth that in 1770 Willenhall contained 148 locksmiths, Wolverhampton 134, and Bilston 8; while nearly a century later, in 1855, the numbers were Willenhall 340, Wolverhampton 110, and Bilston 2, which shows that the trade grew in Willenhall at the expense of the adjoining places. Yet lockmaking was carried on in Bilston as early as 1590, when the Perrys, the Kempsons, and the Tomkyses, all leading families, were engaged in the trade. In 1796 Isaac Mason, inventor of the "fly press" for making various parts of a lock, migrated from Bilston to Willenhall.

The Willenhall specimen of a miniature lock is thus mentioned in a diary of the Rev. T. Unett, "June 13, 1776, James Lees, of Willenhall, aged 63 years and upwards, showed me a padlock with its key, made by himself, that was not the weight of a silver twopence. He at the same time shewed me a lock that was not the weight of a silver penny; he was then making the key to it, all of iron. He said he would be bound to make a dozen locks, with their keys, that should not exceed the weight of a sixpence."

Before the rise of factories into which workmen might be collected, and their labour more healthily regulated, Willenhall lock-making was always conducted in small domiciliary workshops. Had any one at the close of the eighteenth century peeped in at the grimy little windows of one of these low-roofed workshops, and made himself acquainted with the extreme dirtiness of the calling, he would scarcely have ventured to regard it as one befitting the dainty hands of the highest personage of the most fastidious of nations. Yet that unfortunate monarch, Louis XVI., prided himself not on his statesmanship, but upon his skill as a practical locksmith, and his intimacy with all the intricacies of the craft. He had fitted up in his palace at the Tuileries a forge with hearth and anvil, bellows and bench, from which it was his delight to turn out with his own hands all kinds of work in the shape of "spring, double bolt, or catch lock."

> He smokes his forge, he bares his sinewy arm,
> And bravely pounds the sounding anvil warm.

Locks of every variety of principle and quality are produced in Willenhall; the chief kinds being the cabinet lock, the best qualities of which range from 10s. to £3 each, while the commoner ones are sold at from 10s. to 3s. the dozen; the rim lock for doors having two or three bolts, and opening with knob and key; the stock or fine plate lock, imbedded in a wooden case to stand the weather when used on exposed yard or stable doors; the drawback lock for hill doors, with a spring bolt that can be worked from the inside with a knob or from the outside with a latch-key; the dead lock, having one large bolt worked by the key, but not catching or springing like the rim lock; the mortice lock, which is buried in the door, and may be of the dead, the rim, or the drawback variety; the familiar loose padlock made in immense quantities both of iron and of brass; and others less familiar.

The lock-producing centre includes Wolverhampton, Willenhall, Wednesfield, and some of the outlying rural districts like Brewood and Pendeford, where parts and fittings are prepared. In the mother parish the business is extensive and extending; at Wednesfield, iron cabinets and till locks, as well as various kinds of keys, are produced in great numbers, for keys are frequently made apart from the locks as a separate branch of the trade.

Willenhall produces most of the same kinds as Wolverhampton, except the fine plate, though oftener in the cheaper qualities; rim locks are very largely made, all on the Carpenter and Young patent, most of them for export. Willenhall locks are all warded, the wards varying in strength and complexity, known as common, fine round, sash, and solid wards.

It was the Carpenter and Young invention of 1830, making the action of the catch bolt perpendicular instead of horizontal, which renewed the vitality of the town's staple industry.

As registered the patent was entered:—

> "No. 5,880, 18 January, 1830. James Carpenter, of
> Willenhall, and John Young, of Wolverhampton,
> locksmiths. Improvements in locks."

Mr. R. B. Prosser, a recognised authority on patents and inventions, records that in 1841 Carpenter brought an action against one Smith, but the verdict was given for the defendant, it being held that Carpenter's lock was not a new invention (Webster's Reports of Patent Cases, Vol. I., p. 530).

Notwithstanding this the lock has always been known, and is still known, as "Carpenter's lift-up lock."

James Carpenter, the founder of the business still carried on under the style of Carpenter and Tildesley, was not a native of Willenhall. His first place of business was in Walsall Street opposite the "Wake Field"; thence he removed to Stafford Street, occupying the premises now the Three Crowns Inn; subsequently building and occupying the Summerford Works (and Summerford House) in the New Road, where the concern is still carried on James Carpenter, the patentee, was a keen man of business, and distinguished for great decision of character. His daughter Harriet married James Tildesley, who became a partner in the business. Carpenter died in 1844, and Tildesley in 1876, and the concern has since been carried on by the two eldest sons of the latter in partnership, James Carpenter Tildesley (who is now permanently invalided, and of whom more anon), and Clement Tildesley. Mr. Clement Tildesley, who, like his brother, is a county magistrate, still lives at Summerford House, where he was born.

Mr. Rowland Tildesley, solicitor, and Clerk to the Willenhall Urban District Council, is the fourth son of James Tildesley.

James Tildesley's eldest daughter, Louisa Elizabeth, married William Henry Hartill, surgeon, and J.P. for the county of Stafford, who died in 1889; his second daughter, Emily, married John Thomas Hartill, J.P., surgeon, who filled the office of President of the Staffordshire Branch of the British Medical Association in 1885, and again in 1907.

With these few biographical details of Willenhall's chief inventor we pass on.

Other local patents in this branch of industry on the Register are:—

No. 8543—13th June, 1840—Joseph Wolverson, locksmith, William Rawlett, latch maker, both of Willenhall. "Locks and latches."

No. 8903—29 March, 1841.—James Tildesley, of Willenhall, factor, and Joseph Sanders, of Wolverhampton, Lock manufacturer. "Locks."

No. 10611—15th April, 1845.—George Carter, of Willenhall, jobbing smith. "Locks and latches.

No. 12604—8th May, 1849.—Samuel Wilkes, of Wednesfield Heath, brass founder. "Knobs, handles, and spindles for the same, and locks."

[There are patents in the name of Samuel Wilkes, at Darlaston, ironfounder, in 1840, for hinges; and for vices in the same year. In 1851, Samuel Wilkes, of Wolverhampton, iron founder, took out a patent for hinges. In 1845, Samuel Wilkes, of Wolverhampton, brass founder, took out a patent for kettles. The Wilkes' family hereabouts are manifestly as ingenious as they are numerous.]

At the present time there are some 90 factories and 143 workshop employers in Willenhall, besides nine factories and 47 workshops in the Short Heath district. The most important firms in the lock trade are Messrs. Carpenter and Tildesley, H. and T. Vaughan, William Vaughan, John Minors and Sons, J. Waine and Sons, Beddow and Sturmey, Legge and Chilton, and Enoch Tonks and Sons. In the casting trades are John Harper and Co., Ltd. (by far the largest concern), Wm. Harper, Son, and Co., C. and L. Hill, H. and J. Hill, T. Pedley, H. and T. Vaughan (under the style of D. Knowles and Sons), and Arthur Tipper. In this branch of the industry women are largely employed, and children to a slight extent, in attending to light hand and power presses. Female labour is now utilised in the making of parts of machine-made locks (a method of production introduced during the last generation), and for varnishing, painting, and bronzing both the machine and the hand-made goods.

The rate of wages for workmen in the lock trade now ranges from 20s. to 35s. per week, yielding an average of about 29s. Of the wares produced there are probably 300 varieties, many of them in several sizes each, the gross output running into thousands of dozens per week, and so great is their diversity that they range from field padlocks to ponderous prison locks, and the selling prices vary from 1d. to 30s. each. They are exported all over the world, finding good markets in Australasia and South Africa.

Tradition forbids that we should omit here the two stock illustrations of the fact that lock-making ranks among the notoriously ill-paid industries. One is the familiar exaggeration that if a Willenhall locksmith happens to let fall the lock he is making, he never stoops to pick up because he can make another in less time.

The other is the hackneyed anecdote of the late G. B. Thorneycroft, who was once taunted with the sneer that some padlocks of local manufacture would only lock once; and who promptly retorted that as they had been bought at twopence each, it would be "a shame if they did lock twice" at such starvation prices of production. But Willenhall's contributions to the hardware production of the Black Country are by no means limited to this endless variety of locks, some for doors and gates, some for carpet bags and travelling trunks, some for writing portfolios and jewel caskets; but extends to lock furniture and door furniture, latches, door bolts, hasps and keys, hooks and steel vermin traps, grid-irons and box-iron stands, files and wood-screws, ferrules and iron-tips for Lancashire clogs; and other small oddments of the hardware trade.

The making of currycombs, though shrunk to somewhat insignificant proportions within the last quarter of a century, was once a very prominent industry in Willenhall. In 1815 James Carpenter, whose name is now so prominent in the lock trade, took out a patent, which was registered as follows:—

> No. 3956—23rd August, 1815.—James Carpenter, of Willenhall, curry comb maker. "Improvements to a curry comb, by inverting the handle over the back of the comb, and thus rendering the pressure, when in use, more equal."

Another typical industry was the making of door-bolts, now represented by the firms of Joseph Tipper, and Jonah Banks and Sons. It is interesting to note that among the last of the old trade tokens circulating in this locality, were the Willenhall farthings issued by Austin, a miller, baker, and grocer, who carried on business at the corner of Stafford Street (the same now conducted by Joshua Rushbrooke); the obverse of this coin bore as a design characteristic of the town a padlock, a currycomb, and a door-bolt, with the legend, "Let Willenhall flourish," and the date 1844.

The Currycomb manufacture is now represented by D. Ferguson, and by W. H. Tildesley, the latter adding to it the making of steel traps.

But whatever loss has been incurred by the shrinkage of this industry has been more than made up by the enormous growth of the trade in stampings—keys are stamped—and in malleable castings.

The earliest Willenhall patent was taken out in this branch of trade, and thus specified: "No. 3,800. 7th April, 1814. Isaac Mason, Willenhall, tea tray maker. Making stamped front for register stoves and other stoves, fenders, tea trays, and other trays, mouldings, and other articles, in brass and other metals."

In the stamping trades at the present time are Messrs. Armstrong, Stevens and Co., Vaughan Brothers, Alexander Lloyd and Sons, Baxter, Vaughan, and Co., and J. B. Brooks and Co. At the works of Messrs. John Harper and Co., by far the largest in the town, a variety of hardware articles are produced, besides locks, but the bulk of their trade is in the production of castings, especially in the form of gas and oil stoves and lamps. New developments continue to bring in fresh industries.

XXVIII.—Willenhall in Fiction.

A vivid picture of the social and industrial conditions which formerly prevailed in this locality has been drawn by the masterly pen of Disraeli, who evidently studied this side of the Black Country at close quarters. It occurs in his novel, "Sybil," the time of action being about 1837.

The distinguished novelist discovered the well-known fact that many of the common people hereabout were ignorant of their own names, and that if they knew them few indeed were able to spell them. Of nicknames, which were then not merely prevalent, but practically universal, he gives us such choice examples as Devilsdust, Chatting Jack, and Dandy Mick; while in "Shuttle and Screw's Mill," and the firm of "Truck and Trett," we recognise names significant of the methods of employment then in vogue.

But worse perhaps than the "truck system" of paying wages in kind instead of in coin, was the prevailing system of utilising an inordinate number of apprentices; and as these were almost invariably "parish apprentices," the output of the local workhouses, the tendency was not only to lower the rate of wages, but to lower the morale of the people.

How this tendency worked out in everyday life is best seen in the following extract from "Sybil." Under the fictional name "Wemsbury" may perhaps be read Wednesbury; "Hell House Yard" is evidently meant for Hell Lane, near Sedgley; and as to "Wodgate," there can be no doubt about its interpretation as Wednesfield. This is Disraeli's description of life here seventy years ago, no doubt viewed as it was approached from the Wolverhampton side:—

> Wodgate, or Wogate, as it was called on the map, was a district that in old days had been consecrated to Woden, and which appeared destined through successive ages to retain its heathen character.

> At the beginning of the revolutionary war Wodgate was a sort of squatting district of the great mining region to which it was contiguous, a place where adventurers in the industry which was rapidly developed settled themselves; for though the great veins of coal and ironstone cropped up, as they phrase it, before they reached this bare and barren land, and it was thus deficient in those mineral and metallic treasures which had enriched its neighbourhood, Wodgate had advantages of its own, and of a kind which touch the fancy of the lawless.

It was land without an owner; no one claimed any manorial right over it; they could build cottages without paying rent. It was a district recognised by no parish; so there were no tithes and no meddlesome supervision. It abounded in fuel which cost nothing, for though the veins were not worth working as a source of mining profit, the soil of Wodgate was similar in its superficial character to that of the country around.

So a population gathered, and rapidly increased in the ugliest spot in England, to which neither Nature nor art had contributed a single charm; where a tree could not be seen, a flower was unknown, where there was neither belfry nor steeple, nor a single sight or sound that could soften the heart or humanize the mind.

Whatever may have been the cause, whether, as not unlikely, the original squatters brought with them some traditionary skill, or whether their isolated and unchequered existence concentrated their energies on their craft, the fact is certain, that the inhabitants of Wodgate early acquired a celebrity as skilful workmen.

This reputation so much increased, and in time spread so far, that, for more than a quarter of a century, both in their skill and the economy of their labour, they have been unmatched throughout the country.

As manufacturers of ironmongery they carry the palm from the whole district; as founders of brass and workers of steel they fear none; while as nailers and locksmiths, their fame has spread even to the European markets whither their most skilful workmen have frequently been invited.

Invited in vain! No wages can tempt the Wodgate man from his native home, that squatters' seat which soon assumed the form of a large village, and then in turn soon expanded into a town, and at the present moment numbers its population by swarming thousands, lodged in the most miserable tenements, in the most hideous burgh, in the ugliest country in the world.

But it has its enduring spell. Notwithstanding the spread of its civic prosperity, it has lost none of the characteristics of its original society; on the contrary, it has zealously preserved them. There are no landlords, head-lessees, main-masters, or butties in Wodgate.

No church there has yet raised its spire; and, as if the jealous spirit of Woden still haunted his ancient temple, even the conventicle scarcely dare show his humble front in some obscure corner. There is no municipality, no magistrate; there are no local acts, no vestries, no schools of any kind. The streets are never cleaned; every man lights his own house; nor does any one know anything except his business.

More than this, at Wodgate, a factory or large establishment of any kind is unknown. Here Labour reigns supreme. Its division, indeed, is favoured by their manners, but the interference or influence of mere capital is instantly resisted.

The business of Wodgate is carried on by master workmen in their own houses, each of whom possess an unlimited number of what they call apprentices, by whom their affairs are principally conducted, and whom they treat as the Mamlouks treated the Egyptians.

These master workmen indeed form a powerful aristocracy, nor is it possible to conceive one apparently more oppressive. They are ruthless tyrants; they habitually inflict upon their subjects punishments more grievous than the slave population of our colonies were ever visited with; not content with beating them with sticks, or flogging them with knotted ropes, they are in the habit of felling them with, or cutting their heads open with a file or lock.

The most usual punishment, however, or rather stimulus to increase exertion, is to pull an apprentice's ears till they run with blood. These youths, too, are worked for sixteen or even twenty hours a day; they are often sold by one master to another; they are fed on carrion, and they sleep in lofts or cellars.

Yet, whether it be that they are hardened by brutality, and really unconscious of their degradation and unusual sufferings, or whether they are supported by the belief that their day to be masters and oppressors will surely arrive, the aristocracy of Wodgate is by no means so unpopular as the aristocracy of most other places.

In the first place, it is a real aristocracy; it is privileged, but it does something for its privileges. It is distinguished from the main body, not merely by name. It is the most knowing class at Wodgate; it possesses, in deed, in its way, complete knowledge; and it imparts in its manner a certain quantity of it to those whom it guides.

Thus it is an aristocracy that leads, and therefore a fact. Moreover, the social system of Wodgate is not an unvarying course of infinite toil. Their plan is to work hard, but not always. They seldom exceed four days of labour in the week. On Sunday the masters begin to drink; for the apprentices there is dog-fighting without any stint.

On Monday and Tuesday the whole population of Wodgate is drunk; of all stations, ages, and sexes, even babes who should be at the breast, for they are drammed with

Godfrey's cordial. Here is relaxation, excitement; if less vice otherwise than might be at first anticipated, we must remember that excesses are checked by poverty of blood and constant exhaustion. Scanty food and hard labour are in their way, if not exactly moralists, a tolerably good police.

There are no others at Wodgate to preach or to control. It is not that the people are immoral, for immorality implies some forethought; or ignorant, for ignorance is relative; but they are animals, unconscious, their minds a blank, and their worst actions only the impulse of a gross or savage instinct. There are many in this town who are ignorant of their very names; very few who can spell them.

It is rare that you meet with a young person who knows his own age; rarer to find the boy who has seen a book, or the girl who has seen a flower. Ask them the name of their Sovereign, and they will give you an unmeaning stare; ask them the name of their religion, and they will laugh; who rules them on earth, or who can save them in Heaven, are alike mysteries to them.

Such was the population with whom Morley was about to mingle. Wodgate had the appearance of a vast squalid suburb. As you advanced, leaving behind you long lines of little dingy tenements, with infants lying about the road, you expected every moment to emerge into some streets, and encounter buildings bearing some correspondence, in their size and comfort, to the considerable population swarming and busied around you.

Nothing of the kind. There were no public buildings of any sort; no churches, chapels, town hall, institute, theatre; and the principal streets in the heart of the town in which were situate the coarse and grimy shops, though formed by houses of a greater elevation than the preceding, were equally narrow, and, if possible, more dirty.

At every fourth or fifth house, alleys, seldom above a yard wide, and streaming with filth, opened out of the street. These were crowded with dwellings of various size, while from the principal court often branched out a number of smaller alleys, or rather narrow passages, than which nothing can be conceived more close and squalid and obscure.

> Here, during the days of business, the sound of the hammer and the file never ceased, amid gutters of abomination, and piles of foulness; and stagnant pools of filth, reservoirs of leprosy and plague, whose exhalations were sufficient to taint the atmosphere of the whole kingdom, and fill the country with fever and pestilence.

Such were the conditions of life in Willenhall, at least from the industrial side; for Willenhall and Wednesfield were at that time almost identical in their industrial, social, and municipal economics. The novelist is, of course, incorrect in saying Wednesfield had no church; as we have seen in Chapter XXIII. it had possessed a small church or chapel since 1746.

Another novelist who has dealt with the same theme is Louis Becke. The hero of his tale, entitled "Old Convict Days" (published by T. Fisher Unwin), is a runaway apprentice from Darlaston; and Willenhall is alluded to in this work as "Wilnon." Spirited descriptions are given of regular set fights between the apprentices of the two towns, which took place on the canal bridge that divided their respective territories near Bug Hole, and in the course of which drownings have not been unknown to occur. Allusions are also made to the dog-fighting, human rat worrying, and other brutal sports with which the populace of these two places were wont to amuse themselves; and particularly to the haunted Red Barn in which a murder had been committed.

Willenhall can lay a further claim to classic ground in the realm of fiction, though the exact spot has not yet been satisfactorily identified. It is the place called Mumper's Dingle, in the works of George Borrow, the gipsy traveller and linguist, or as he calls himself in the Romany dialect, Lavengro, the "Word-Master."

The word "mumper" signifies a tramp or roving beggar; but its slight likeness to the name Monmer has led certain local enthusiasts to identify Mumpers' Dingle with Monmer Lane. Wherever this particular gipsies' dingle may have been, it was certainly on the Essington side of Willenhall, though scarcely five miles out; in fact, the public-house mentioned in the narrative ("Lavengro," chapter 89) is generally understood to be the Bull's Head Inn, Wolverhampton Street, which is definitely stated to be two miles from Mumpers' Dingle. It must have been a secluded and romantic spot about the year 1820, and quite a fitting scene for that interesting episode of the gipsy life described as being led there by the unconventional Lavengro, in Platonic association with a strapping Gitano wench named Isopel Berners.

Since George Borrow has come to be recognised as a writer fitting to rank among our standard English authors, quite a Borrovian cult has grown up, which has naturally enough fortified itself by a literature of its own.

Our first extracts are the great writer's own description of the place. ("Isopel Berners," by George Borrow.)

> The Dingle is a deep, wooded, and, consequently, somewhat gloomy hollow in the middle of a very large, desolate field. The shelving sides of the hollow are overgrown with trees and bushes. A belt of sallows crowns the circular edge of the small crater. At the lowest part of the Dingle are discovered a stone and a fire of charcoal, from which spot a winding path ascends to "the plain." On either side of the fire is a small encampment. One consists of a small pony cart and a small hut-shaped tent, occupied by the Word-Master, on the other side is erected a kind of tent, consisting of large hoops covered over with tarpaulin, quite impenetrable to rain; hard by stands a small donkey cart. This is "the tabernacle" of Isopel Berners. A short distance off, near a spring of clear water, is the encampment of the Romany chals and chies—the Petulengres and their small clan.

The place is above five miles from Willenhall, in Staffordshire.

The time is July, 1825.

Our concluding quotation is taken from the "Life, Writings, and Correspondence of George Borrow," by William J. Knapp (published in 1899).

> 1825.
>
> On the 21st, he departs with his itinerant hosts towards the old Welsh border—Montgomery. Turns back with Ambrose Petulengro. Settles in Mumber Lane, Staffordshire, near Willenhall. My informant of Dudley caused it to be found, and wrote as follows:—
>
> "'Mumpers' Dingle' still exists in the neighbourhood of Willenhall, though it does not seem to be well known, as a native had to make inquiries about it. Willenhall itself is one of the most forlorn-looking places in the Black Country, ranking second to Darlaston, I should think."

XXIX.—Bibliography.

From the merely allusive in literature, we proceed to the bibliography of Willenhall, which, though not extensive, is of fair average interest.

Recently (June, 1907) was put up for auction in London a First Folio Shakespeare of some local interest. It was the property of Mr. Abel Buckley, Ryecroft Hall, near Manchester. This folio appears to have been purchased about 1660 by Colonel John Lane, of Bentley Hall, Staffs, the protector of Charles II. after the Battle of Worcester. It remained in the possession of the family till 1856, when, at the dispersal of the library of Colonel John Lane, of King's Bromley, whose book-plate, designed by Hogarth, is inserted, it was bought by the third Earl of Gosford for 157 guineas.

The son of the third Earl of Gosford disposed of it to James Toovey, the famous London bookseller, for £470 in 1884; and soon afterwards Mr. Buckley obtained the folio. It measures 12⅞in. by 8¼in., is throughout clean, but the fly-leaf and title are mounted and two leaves repaired. This is the volume's interesting history, according to Mr. Sidney Lee.

In 1795, Stephen Chatterton, a Willenhall schoolmaster, published a book of poems of a humorous cast. One is "An epistle to my friend Mr. Thomas S—, who was married in July, 1783, to his third wife, on his fiftieth birthday."

The bibliography of the Rev. Samuel Cozens, at one time minister of the Peculiar Baptists' Chapel at Little London, Willenhall, is rather extensive if not very interesting. A full list of his pamphlets and other works will be found in G. T. Lawley's "Bibliography of Wolverhampton," and also in Simms' "Bibliotheca Staffordiensis." His first work, which appeared in the "Gospel Standard," 1844, was "A short account of the Lord's Gracious Dealings with One of the Elect Vessels of Mercy," and is autobiographical.

From this title, and that of the second part of his life, which appeared in 1857, "Reminiscences: or Footsteps of Providence," the attitude of mind assumed by the writer may be easily guessed. His was a dogmatic creed, of stern unyielding Calvinism, which left him always self-satisfied, and often made him aggressive. He moved from Wolverhampton to Willenhall in 1848, where his first book was written, a scholarly volume in the form of "A Biblical Lexicon."

Presently his combative nature found expression in a controversial pamphlet attacking the Primitive Methodists, "John Wesley, the Papa of British Rome, and Philip Pugh, the modern Pelagius, weighed in the Balance of Eternal Truth and found wanting" (Willenhall, printed and published by W. H. Hughes, 1852). The Rev. Philip Pugh was located at Darlaston, and made a gallant defence on behalf of his co-religionists; the Primitive Methodists of

Willenhall acknowledging these services by presenting him with a handsome testimonial. The pamphlets containing his rejoinders bear the imprint of Stephen Hackett, Willenhall. Mr. Cozens died in Tasmania some years later.

The "Memoirs of G. B. Thorneycroft," written by the Rev. J. B. Owen, and published (Wolverhampton: T. Simpson) in 1856, contain local allusions of minor interest. The subject of the memoir was the well-known South Staffordshire ironmaster, who in the earlier part of his commercial career had some works near the Waterglade, on the Bilston Road.

George Benjamin Thorneycroft, was born August 20th, 1791, at Tipton, where his grandfather kept the Three Furnaces Inn. His biographer claims his descent from the Thornicrofts of Cheshire. In his youth he was employed at Kirkstall Forge, near Leeds, returning to Staffordshire in 1809 to work at the Moorcroft Ironworks at Bradley, near Bilston, where, by his skill and industry he ultimately rose to the management.

It was in 1817 he founded a small ironwork at Willenhall, and seven years later joined his twin brother, Edward Thorneycroft, in establishing the Shrubbery Ironworks at Wolverhampton. The rise of the railways at that period, and the consequent larger demands for iron and steel, were among the causes which led to his great prosperity as an ironmaster.

His Willenhall residence was on the site now occupied by the Metropolitan Bank, in the Market Place: while his works, this first this iron magnate owned, were located near what is now known as Forge Yard, Waterglade Street. It was in this house his son, Colonel Thorneycroft, of Tettenhall Towers, was born.

His prominence as a public man may be estimated by the fact that when Wolverhampton was incorporated in 1848, Mr. Thorneycroft was selected for the honour of being first Mayor of the new borough. He was at all times a generous supporter of every local charity and benevolent institution, till the old quotation came to be fitted to him:—

> There was a man—the neighbours thought him mad—
> The more he gave away, the more he had.

In the Town Hall of Wolverhampton a statue has been set up to commemorate the public work of this estimable character.

Although during the greater portion of his career a great supporter of the State Church, in earlier life Mr. G. B. Thorneycroft had been an ardent Wesleyan; and in his memoirs (p. 134) it is recorded how he liquidated the burden of debt on the Willenhall Chapel belonging to that denomination. On his death, in 1851, among those who testified to his public usefulness, and the estimation in which he was held, was the Rev. G. H. Fisher, of Willenhall (memoirs pp. 263–5).

"The Willenhall Magazine" was the name of a monthly periodical launched in 1862, "published for the proprietors by J. Loxton, Market Place, Willenhall," and having Messrs. J. C. and Jesse Tildesley as its chief contributors. The first number appeared in March, and twelve months afterwards this praiseworthy attempt to establish a local magazine in Willenhall had completely failed.

In 1866 appeared a religious novel written by a Primitive Methodist preacher of this town, and published by Elliot Stock, London. It: was entitled "Nest: A Tale of the Early British Christians," by the Rev. J. Boxer, Willenhall. Mr. G. T. Lawley describes it as a well-written story dealing with the pagan persecution of the early British Christians by their Saxon conquerors.

A story of direct local interest was Mr. G. T. Lawley's work "The Locksmith's Apprentice; a Tale of Old Willenhall," published serially some years ago in the columns of a Wolverhampton weekly newspaper.

Mr N. Neal Solly (of the firm of Fletcher, Solly, and Urwick, Willenhall Furnaces) wrote the Guide to the Fine Arts Section of the South Staffordshire Exhibition, held at Molineux House, Wolverhampton, in 1869. The writer was himself an artist, and he afterwards produced some valuable Memoirs of David Cox (1873), and of the Bristol painter, William James Muller (1875).

The most eminent litterateur Willenhall has produced is Mr. James Carpenter Tildesley, a lock manufacturer, as we have seen, and a life-long public man in the town. Reference has already been made to his writings on industrial subjects, and also to his works on the history of local Methodism. As a public man, he is a Justice of the Peace for the County, a chairman of Willenhall Petty Sessional Division, has been president of the Wolverhampton Chamber of Commerce, chairman of the Willenhall Local Board, and chairman of the Willenhall Liberal Association. Since his retirement to Penkridge he has written a history of that parish, which was published by Steen and Co., of Wolverhampton, in 1886.

Mr. J. C. Tildesley was sub-editor of the "Birmingham Morning News" under the famous George Dawson, and has been a most diligent contributor to the Press for the last forty years. It was mainly by his efforts that the Willenhall Literary Institute was founded, that what is now the Public Hall was built, and that the Free Library was established.

In recognition of his work in connection with the Literary Institute, a public presentation was made to him, the inscription upon which bore this eloquent testimony—"Not to requite but to record services of great value to Willenhall . . . January 4th, 1869." That Mr. J. C. Tildesley is now permanently invalided is a matter of regret not only to Willenhall, but to a wide circle of readers and admirers outside the township.

XXX.—Topography.

There is often a wealth of history to be unearthed from place-names. Localities often preserve the names of dead and gone personages, half-forgotten incidents, and matters of past history well worth recalling for their interest. Besides the pleasure to be derived from the right interpretation of place-names and old street names, great interest often centres around the social associations of old inns and taverns. Let us consider a few of the old-time inns and localities of Willenhall.

The site of the mediæval Holy Well, which in the later fashion of the 18th century blossomed forth as a Spa, was situated between the church and the present Manor House. In the remoter age we may imagine it as the haunt of the lame, the halt, and the blind (possibly the church was dedicated to St. Giles, the patron of cripples, on this account), and in the more recent period as the resort of fashionable invalids and wealthy valetudinarians.

In the Private Act of Parliament, dated 6th August, 1844, for disposing of the Willenhall Endowment properties, a number of field-names occur in the schedule which are pregnant with local history. Welch End is a name which seems to mark the locality where resided the family of Welch, who founded the church dole; the Doctor's Piece was perhaps part of the estate of the celebrated Dr. Wilkes; the Clothers and the Little Clothiers are names which are said to indicate certain lands once belonging to the Cloth-workers' Company of the City of London; Somerford Bridge Piece and the Hither Bathing were presumably located near the brook; while the Poor's Piece, the Constable's Dole, and the Dole's Butty (query: does the last-named, interpreted in the dialect of the district, signify "the companion piece to the Dole?"), are names which suggest the identity of charity lands.

There is mention of a High Causeway, which manifestly indicates the position of some old paved road; and the Butts, doubtless, named the field where in ancient times archery was practised by the men of Willenhall, as the men of Darlaston did at the Butcroft in their parish.

Reverting to the schedule, there are some names for which no explanation can be offered; as Ell Park, Berry Stile, the Stringes, and the Farther Stringes. Many of the properties named in the list are declared to be "uninclosed lands that lie dispersedly in the Common Fields there, intermixed with other lands." How much, or rather, how little, common land is there in Willenhall to-day?

And yet the amount of "waste" land in and around Willenhall was once excessive, as the writings of George Borrow cannot fail to convey (Chap. XXVIII.). In Chap. XXII. we read of Canne Byrch, situated in "Willenhall

Field," lying in the highway towards Darlaston, where perhaps the village community of ancient times tilled their lands in common; and more directly of the "waste or common land" called Shepwell Green; a wide stretch of open land once apparently stretching away towards the wilderness and solitudes of that gipsy-land immortalised by George Borrow.

"Willenhall Green" is named by Dr. Plot, writing in 1686, as a place where yellow ochre was found a yard below the surface, and which after being beaten up was made into oval cakes to be sold at fourpence a dozen to glovers, who used it in combination with cakes of "blew clay," found at Darlaston and Wednesbury, "for giving their wares an ash colour."

The old highway between Walsall and Wolverhampton lay along Walsall Street, through Cross Street, and the Market Place; the new coach route, or the New Road, as it was called, was made in the early part of the nineteenth century.

New Invention is a place-name which originated not from any connection with the local industries, as one might be led to expect, but from nothing more serious than a nickname of derision. The tradition is that many years ago an inhabitant from the centre of the town was strolling out that way, when he was thus accosted by an acquaintance living in one of the few cottages which then comprised the neighbourhood, and who was standing on his own doorstep to enjoy the cool of the evening: "I say, Bill, hast seen my new invention?" "No, lad; what is it?" "That's it!" said the self-satisfied householder, pointing up to a hawthorn bush which was pushed out of the top of his chimney. "That's it! It's stopped our o'd chimdy smokin', I can tell thee!" And ever after that the locality which this worthy honoured with his ingenious presence was slyly dubbed by his amused neighbours the "New Invention," by which name it afterwards became generally known.

Portobello, on the outskirts of Willenhall, is said to have borrowed its name from that second-hand Portobello near Leith, which was named after Admiral Vernon's famous victory of 1739. At the Scottish suburb a bed of rich clay, discovered in 1765, led to the development of the place through the establishment of brick and tile works; a similar discovery of a thick bed of clay outside Willenhall, and its subsequent industrial development on parallel lines led to the copying of that patriotic name, more particularly because a neighbouring coal-pit was already rejoicing in the name of Bunker's Hill, conferred upon it by local patriots after the American victory of 1775. The Willenhall wags, however, have given quite another derivation. A man once passing a solitary farmhouse in that locality, say they, called and inquired if the farmer had any beer on tap. The reply was, as the man pointed cellarwards, "No—only porter below!"

Little London seems to be a locality which attempts to shine by the reflected glory of the capital's borrowed name, and is appropriately approached by a thoroughfare called Temple Bar; but which of these metropolitan names suggested the other, the oldest inhabitant fails to recollect.

Among the old inns and taverns of the town the chief were the Neptune Inn, Walsall Street; the Bull's Head, Wolverhampton Street; the Hope and Anchor, Little London; the Bell Inn, Market Place; and the Waterglade Tavern, Waterglade. The Neptune, situated on the main road between Wolverhampton and Walsall, and almost opposite the church, was formerly a posting-house kept in the 18th and early part of the 19th century by Isaac Hartill, one of those typical hosts of the coaching period; active, genial, and obliging, a man of good conversational powers, and one who instantly made his guests feel at home, and was extremely popular with all the local gentry and regular travellers along the road. With the advent of the railway the character of the Neptune Inn gradually altered—the railway, by the way, was cut through the crescent, overlooking Bentley Hall, a property which had belonged to and had been the residence of the Hartill family since 1704, and part of which is now The Robin Hood Grounds, used for sports and recreations and other out-door assemblies.

It was from the balcony above the entry of the Neptune Inn, over which was then the public drawing-room, that the Right Hon. Charles P. Villiers first addressed the electors of the newly-enfranchised borough of Wolverhampton in 1835, and subsequently made many of his fervent Free Trade speeches; and in fact, from this place all public announcements were wont to be made. The room behind the balcony was formerly used as a Court Room, in which the magistrates administered justice; here too, the Willenhall Court Leet was held, and to this day Lord Barnard's agents receive the tithes there.

The Neptune once served all the purposes of a lending inn as an acknowledged place of public rendezvous; and when the Stowheath farmers were accustomed to ride or drive in to attend church, its spacious stableyard was a scene of animation, even on Sundays.

The Bell Inn, in the Market Place, is perhaps the oldest in the market taverns, though the date 1660 painted upon its sign can scarcely refer to the projecting wing which bears it. The back portion of the house is unquestionably old; in fact, the family of Wakelam who kept the inn 25 years ago, were identified with this house and the Bull's Head Inn for upwards of two centuries.

The Plough Inn, Stafford Street, is less old than the others, and of more doubtful interest. It has been completely altered within recent years; in the old days when prisoners consigned to Stafford Gaol had to walk, it was the place of the final drink before starting, and marked the limits of the town till Little London began.

The Bull's head Inn, Wolverhampton Street, is supposed to be the alehouse referred to in Borrow's romantic tale of Romany life, "Lavengro."

The Waterglade Tavern marked the spot on the road between the two old-world villages of Willenhall and Bilston, where it dipped to the bed of the stream.

The Woolpack Inn, at Short Heath, is one of the oldest licensed houses in that locality.

The First and Last Inn, New Invention, was so dubbed because at one time it was the first licensed house when approaching from Wednesfield, and the last when going the other way out.

The sign rhymes of Willenhall belong to the hackneyed type. The Gate Inn, New Invention, has the well-known couplet:—

> This Gate hangs well and hinders none:
> Refresh and pay and travel on.

The Lame Dog Inn, at Short Heath, is not very original with:—

> Step in, my friends, and stop a while,
> To help a lame dog over the stile.

Enough has been said on the subject to arouse the interest of patriotic Willenhaleans. One reflection in conclusion—in the old days licensed houses were invariably kept by families of position and substance, and it is remarkable to discover the great number of professional and well-to-do men of the present day who were born in public-houses. It is so with regard to Wednesbury and Darlaston, and even more so with regard to Willenhall.

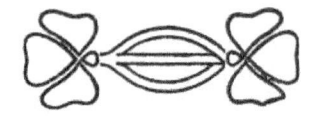

XXXI.—Old Families and Names of Note.

To not a few of the old names of those who have lived their lives in Willenhall, and left their mark indelibly fixed upon its annals, attention has already been paid in treating of the various matters with which their respective life-work was associated. It remains here only to add a few more names to our list of Willenhall worthies, and to supplement a few biographical details to those already mentioned.

The index to the names of landowners would be incomplete without that of Offley. In the year 1555 Alderman Offley, a citizen of London, acquired lands in "Willenhall, otherwise Wilnall." About the same date this opulent merchant became lord of the manor of Darlaston. (See History of Darlaston, pp. 39–40.)

An important old Willenhall family, as may have been gathered in the course of these Annals, was that of Hincks. Their family residence still stands in Bilston Street, near to the Market Place; a descendant, and apparently the only representative of the Hincks family surviving is Mrs. Samuel Walker, of Bentley Hall.

Of Carpenter, Willenhall's most famous inventor, a few more items of local and biographical interest are forthcoming. In early life James Carpenter was a Churchman, but, as many other Willenhall folk did, became a Wesleyan in consequence of the scandals caused by the Rev. Mr. Moreton's mode of life. His remains lie in a vault on the east side of the Wesleyan Chapel in Union Street. He was a keen supporter of the Right Hon. C. P. Villiers when he first became a Parliamentary candidate for Wolverhampton.

John Austin, the tradesman, who first issued the "Willenhall farthings," mentioned in Chapter XXVII., was an enterprising tradesman, a man of handsome presence and of an alert mind. On leaving Willenhall he went to live at Manor House, Allscott, near Wellington, at which town he established artificial manure works, and where he manufactured sulphuric acid very extensively.

The issue of the Willenhall trade farthings was continued by Rushbrooke, his successor in the business (1853), though the original date, "1844" was always retained upon them. They were sold to shopkeepers and traders all round the district at the rate of 5s. nominal for 4s. 9d. cash. When the new national bronze coinage came into circulation in 1860, large quantities of these copper farthing tokens were returned on to Mr Rushbrooke's hands, but he melted them down without sustaining the least loss.

The Hartill family has long been settled in Willenhall. George Hartill married Isabel Cross, at St. Peter's Church, Wolverhampton, in 1662. All their nine children were baptised at St. Giles's Church, Willenhall. The present Dr. J. T. Hartill is descended directly from Richard, fifth son of the above, and his grandfather, Isaac Hartill, inter-married with Ann Hartill, a descendant of the said George Hartill's second son.

The social rank of the Hartills since their residence in Willenhall has been that of tradesmen or professional men, manufacturers, or small property owners, but always educated up to the standard of the period in which they lived. In 1826 Jeremiah Hartill established himself in medical practice, joined in 1861 by his nephew, William Henry Hartill, and in 1869 by the latter's brother, Dr. J. T. Hartill. The arms and crest borne by the last-named were formally granted him in 1896; but the same coat without the crest had always been used by his uncle Jeremiah, and that on a claim of inheritance from the ancient lords of the manor of Hartill, in Cheshire, to whom it had been granted by King John. These particular arms have not been officially recorded at the College of Heralds since 1580, but a very similar coat was used by a member of this family in 1703.

The Willenhall Hartills migrated here from the neighbourhood of Kinver, Wolverley, and Kidderminster. There are still Hartills of the old stock resident in the Kinver district, and from them are descended Mrs. Shakespeare, wife of the well-known Birmingham solicitor; and Mrs. Showell, wife of the late Walter Showell, the founder of the eminent firm of Black Country brewers, who was once a Parliamentary candidate for one of the divisions of Birmingham. The Hartills of Kinver are related to the Hartills of Kingsbury, and there has always been a great similarity in the Christian names borne by the old Kingsbury, Kinver, and Willenhall Hartills. The steeple of Polesworth church was built by the last Sir Richard Hartill, 1377–1379, and below the tower battlements is carved upon a large shield the arms of this benefactor, which are identical with those of the late Dr. Jeremiah Hartill of Willenhall.

Mr. Henry Vaughan, the founder of the largest business concern in the town, has done a large amount of public work in various capacities, but chiefly as a magistrate, a member of the defunct School Board, and more recently as a County Councillor.

Among the justices who have sat on the Willenhall Bench and possessed other connections with the place may be mentioned the late N. Neal Solly, ironmaster, two water-colour drawings by whom hang on the walls of the Free Library; the late Rev. G. H. Fisher, who was chairman; R. D. Gough, a brother of the late Colonel Foster Gough, and who married the rich and benevolent Mary Clemson, daughter of John Clemson, a corn miller, of this township; while among the most recent appointments are Clement Tildesley, Thomas Vaughan, and Thomas Kidson. The present Clerk to the Willenhall Bench is Samuel Mills Slater, in succession to his father, the late James Slater, of Bescot Hall.

A memorial tablet to the local men who fell in the Boer War has been erected at the gateway to the Old Cemetery.

XXXII.—Manners and Customs.

The Manners and Customs of the people of Willenhall have been those held in common with the populace of the surrounding parishes, and which have been dealt with too fully in the published writings of Mr. G. T. Lawley to need more than a brief review here.

The seasonal custom of Well Dressing has been alluded to in Chapter XVII., and of Beating the Bounds in Chapter V. Other ancient customs of minor import existed, but space cannot be found to treat them in a general history.

The social calibre of the people a century or so ago may be gauged by a local illustration of the custom of Wife Selling.

This practice was once common enough everywhere, and amongst the ignorant and illiterate in some parts it is still held to be a perfectly legitimate transaction. From the "Annual Register" this local instance has been clipped:—

> "Three men and three women went to the Bell Inn, Edgbaston Street, Birmingham, and made the following singular entry in the toll book which is kept there: August 31, 1773, Samuel Whitehouse, of the Parish of Willenhall, in the county of Stafford, this day sold his wife, Mary Whitehouse, in open market, to Thomas Griffiths, of Birmingham, value one shilling. To take her with all her faults.
>
> (Signed) Samuel Whitehouse.
> Mary Whitehouse.
>
> Voucher, Thomas Buckley, of Birmingham."

The parties were all exceedingly well pleased, and the money paid down for the toll as for a regular purchase.

So much for the moral status of the people; now to consider them from the industrial side.

The older generation of Willenhall men were accustomed, ere factory Acts and kindred forms of parental legislation had regulated working hours and otherwise ameliorated the conditions of labour, to slave for many weary hours in little domiciliary workshops. Boys were then apprenticed at a tender age, and soon became humpbacked in consequence of throwing in the weight of their little bodies in the endeavour to eke out the strength of the feeble thews and bones in their immature arms.

In those days men worked when they liked, and played when it suited them; they generally played the earlier days of the week, even if at the end they worked night and day in the attempt to average the weekly earnings. In this connection it has been suggested that in pre-Reformation times Willenhall folk duly honoured St. Sunday and well as St. Monday, consecrating both days to the sacred cause of weekly idleness. Or was Willenhall's Holy Well dedicated to St. Dominic, and came by grammatical error to be called St. Sunday? As thus—Sanctus Dominicus abbreviated first to Sanc. Dominic, and then extended in the wrong gender to Sancta Dominica, otherwise Saint Sunday? Who shall say? It may have been so.

It is perhaps in their pleasures, more than in their pursuits, that the character of a people is to be best seen. Allusion has been made to the obsolete Trinity Fair in Chapter XII.; but the Wake has remained to this day, less loyally observed perhaps, but rich in traditions of past glories.

Willenhall Wake falls on the first Sunday after September 11th, the Feast of St. Giles, to whom the old church is dedicated.

Among the wakes of the Black Country none are richer in reminiscence of the old time forms of festivity than that of Willenhall. Although in later times the outward and visible sign of its celebration has dwindled down to an assemblage of shows and roundabouts, shooting galleries, and ginger-bread stalls, it was once accompanied by bull-baitings and cock-fighting, and all the other coarse and brutal sports in which our forefathers so much delighted.

> At Wednesfield at one village wake
>   The cockers all did meet
> At Billy Lane's, the cock-fighter's,
>   To have a sporting treat.
>
> For Charley Marson's spangled cock
>   Was matched to fight a red
> That came from Will'n'all o'er the fields,
>   And belonged to "Cheeky Ned."
>
> Two finer birds in any cock-pit
>   Two never yet was seen.
> Though the Wednesfield men declared
>   Their cock was sure to win.
>
> The cocks fought well, and feathers fled
>   All round about the pit,
> While blood from both of 'em did flow
>   Yet ne'er un would submit.

> At last the spangled Wedgefield bird
>   Began to show defeat,
> When Billy Lane, he up and swore
>   The bird shouldn't be beat;
>
> For he would fight the biggest mon
>   That came from Will'n'all town,
> When on the word, old "Cheeky Ned"
>   Got up and knocked him down.
>
> To fight they went like bull-dogs,
>   As it is very well known,
> Till "Cheeky Ned" seized Billy's thumb,
>   And bit it to the bone.
>
> At this the Wednesfield men begun
>   Their comrade's part to take,
> And never was a fiercer fight
>   Fought at a village wake.
>
> They beat the men from Will'n'all town
>   Back to their town again,
> And long they will remember
>   This Wednesfield wake and main.

The site of the Willenhall Bull Ring, it may be added for the information of future generations, was opposite the Baptist Chapel, Little London, where Temple Bar joins the Wednesfield and Bloxwich Roads.

Among other Wake observances of the last century were the "Club Walkings" or processioning of the Friendly Societies, whose members first attended a brief service in the church, and then spent the rest of the day in feasting at the Neptune Inn opposite. Tradition hath it that further back, well into the Georgian era, and certainly before Mr. Fisher's time, another Wake custom was that of "kissing the parson," a privilege of which the women were said to be very jealous.

In the year 1857 the Right Hon. C. P. Villiers, Member of Parliament for the Borough of Wolverhampton, of which this township was part, inaugurated in Willenhall one of the first exhibitions of fine art and industry ever held in the Black Country. It was opened on the Monday in the Wake week, and Mr. Villiers alluded to the fact that "they met in the midst of one of those old-fashioned wakes which it was the humour of their ancestors to establish and be pleased with," and the right hon. gentleman proceeded to contrast the present with the past conditions of Willenhall Wake-time.

A flourishing Free Library—founded like many another in the face of great local opposition and prejudice—is one of the legacies of that exhibition, from the date of which may be traced the more rational observance of Wake-time.

With the advance of science and art and the spread of popular education, the future prosperity of an ingenious community, like that of the skilled mechanics and deft craftsmen of this township, is assured. Impressed with such certitude it is all but a work of supererogation to echo the patriotic sentiment of the old-time townsfolk—

"LET WILLENHALL FLOURISH!"

THE END.

Footnotes:

[88] Claudy Phillips, as he was popularly called, seems to have been a man of considerable genius, though not without some of the eccentricities which sometimes accompany it. He was well known throughout the county, which he used to traverse dressed at one time in laced clothes, at others in garments which betrayed the low state of his exchequer. When drawn to it by stress of financial embarassment, he was not above playing in the evening at inns, and throwing himself upon the generosity of his audiences there. As to his qualities as a musician, it is said his *forte* was in wild and plaintive melody, dictated by the impulses of his own mind, and subject to none of the ordinary rules of studied compositions; his manipulation of the violin was also distinguished for a rapidity of execution unrivalled in those days. The handsome marble tablet erected to his memory soon after his death, in 1732, by public subscription, shows that he must have been held in considerable estimation by a goodly number of admirers. Indeed, he must have been known to some of the most prominent personages of his time, as the following lines upon him have been variously attributed to Dr. Johnson or to David Garrick:—

> Phillips, whose touch harmonious could remove
> The pangs of guilty power and hapless love,
> Rest here! distrest by poverty no more,
> Here find that calm thou gav'st so oft before!
> Sleep undisturbed within this peaceful shrine,
> Till angels wake thee with a note like thine!

(See also Oliver's "Wolverhampton," pp. 98 and 99.)